BURLINGTON NORTHERN

DIESEL
LOCOMOTIVES

BURLINGTON NORTHERN

DIESEL LOCOMOTIVES

THREE DECADES OF BN POWER

BY PAUL D. SCHNEIDER

KALMBACH PUBLISHING CO.

To my good and stalwart friend, Paul Bergen

Main cover photo: Steve Glischinski
Inset photos: George Drury (far left); Jim Hediger (second from left and far right); J. David Ingles (second from right)
Cover design: Lawrence Luser
Book design: Jane Kremsreiter

Thanks to Mike Kiriazis for research on the BN roster.

Kalmbach Publishing Co.
21027 Crossroads Circle
P.O. Box 1612
Waukesha, WI 53187

Printed in Hong Kong.

**Library of Congress
Cataloging-in-Publication Data**

Schneider, Paul D.
    Burlington Northern Diesel Locomotives:
    Three decades of BN power
    by Paul D. Schneider.
            p.   cm.
    Includes index.
    ISBN 089024-143-0
    1. Diesel locomotives — United States.
    2. Burlington Northern Railroad
    Company. I. Title.
    TJ619.3.B87336 1993
    604.2'66 — dc20   93-2023

PAUL D. SCHNEIDER PHOTOS

CONTENTS

INTRODUCTION / 8

1
RING OUT THE OLD
Let the locomotive retirements begin / 14

2
A STAY OF EXECUTION
BN's rolling locomotive museum / 26

3
DON'T FEAR THE REAPER
Off to that big roundhouse in the sky / 44

4
BIG BOMBERS
Innovations in high-horsepower locomotives / 60

5
REBUILT AND REBORN
Solving medium-horsepower locomotive problems / 84

6
SLUGS AND OTHER ODDITIES
Locomotive-related experiments / 104

7
THE SURVIVORS
Pre-merger units that live on / 116

8
NEVER SAY DIE
E's and F's in the '80s — and beyond / 132

APPENDIX: THE ROSTER / 150

INDEX / 157

PREFACE

I WROTE THIS BOOK for the person interested in the history of Burlington Northern motive power. Of course, any definition of motive power history is open to wide interpretation by railroad hobbyists. In the case of this book, history is shaped by the retirement and development of BN's various locomotives. Here you'll learn the reasons behind BN's retirements and technological developments. You'll also hear from BN officials and railroaders with firsthand experience with BN's locomotives.

While writing this book I kept in mind former *Trains* magazine editor David P. Morgan's approach to writing about locomotives. There are railfans who will pound their fists on their bound copies of *Trains* and declare that history is dates, facts, and other incontrovertible data. Now, there's no doubt that Morgan loved facts and figures about locomotives. But he went beyond simply rehashing hard data. Much of the magic of Morgan's stories can be traced to his highly subjective point of view and the insightful anecdotes he gleaned from railroaders and others who knew the locomotives best. I've attempted to accomplish the same thing with this book. I hope you enjoy it.

PAUL D. SCHNEIDER PHOTO

*A highly subjective
overview of
BN's history*

INTRODUCTION

IT'S DIFFICULT TO understand the history of Burlington Northern's locomotives without understanding something about Burlington Northern itself. Since it's not within the scope of this book to detail three decades of BN history, you may want to check out George H. Drury's "Burlington Northern" listing in *The Train-Watcher's Guide to North American Railroads* [Kalmbach]. In the meantime, here is my own highly subjective overview of the railroad's history:

MARCH 3, 1970: Burlington Northern is created from four predecessor railroads: Chicago, Burlington & Quincy; Great Northern; Northern Pacific; and Spokane, Portland & Seattle. The main nerve of the 23,000-mile railroad stretches from Chicago to the Pacific Northwest (the old GN and NP routes), south

In 1977 RS3 4064 became the last locomotive from the 1970 merger to exchange its predecessor paint scheme for BN green.

PAUL D. SCHNEIDER PHOTO

S.P.&S.
RY.

4064

BN

to a connection with Santa Fe in northern California (via GN and SP&S), from Chicago to Denver (via the old Burlington), and south from Denver to Texas. BN also uses Burlington tracks between Chicago, St. Louis, and Kansas City. To top it off, BN reaches into Canada (over old GN trackage). The railroad makes its headquarters at St. Paul, Minn. The best thing in my opinion is the railroad's locomotive fleet: 1,987 diesels built by four builders (EMD, GE, Baldwin, and Alco) and operating in a rainbow of paint schemes from the predecessor railroads.

1970-1980: A master renumbering and buckets of Cascade green paint help blend BN's locomotives into the system. An explosion of low-sulphur coal traffic in Montana and Wyoming cranks up BN's revenues and paints a smile on the face of BN management and shareholders.

But not all employees from the four predecessor railroads are happy BN campers. Employee relations for much of the '70s are summed up by an old SP&S engineer in Wishram, Wash., grumbling, "This used to be a damned good railroad. But now it's all gone to hell."

1980: BN merges with the St. Louis-San Francisco, otherwise known as the Frisco. BN's route map now extends south from St. Louis and Kansas City to the Gulf of Mexico. In fact, a BN train that operates between Birmingham, Ala., and Portland, Ore., claims the distinction of being the longest freight train run in the country. The Frisco employees I meet shortly before the merger are concerned that BN will chew up the Frisco — and their jobs — after the merger. Instead, Frisco management takes control of BN and begins to change the operations and direction — if not the personality — of the original BN. In 1984 a BN brakeman who started on the railroad prior to the BN-Frisco merger tells me, "This used to be a damned good railroad. But now it's all gone to hell."

1981: BN absorbs the Colorado & Southern, which had been a Burlington subsidiary (hence the "C&S" sublettering on some BN diesels). C&S' Denver-Texas route is transferred to Fort Worth & Denver, which is itself a subsidiary of the Colorado & Southern. The circle is completed on January 1, 1983, when FW&D is also merged into BN. I can't help but wonder if somewhere in Colorado or Texas former C&S and FW&D employees were standing around a yard office muttering, "This used to be a damned good railroad. But now it's all gone to hell."

THE 1980s: BN fights the Chicago & North Western's and Union Pacific's attempt to gain access to the Powder River Basin . . . and loses. The deregulation of the U.S. railroad industry allows BN and other Class 1 railroads to spin off certain railroad lines. BN can now prune unprofitable or marginally profitable branches from its network

so that it can concentrate on traffic moving over its trunk lines. For example, BN spins off 145 miles of ex-Frisco track in Arkansas and Missouri to a group of investors who name the railroad, appropriately enough, the Arkansas & Missouri. Because A&M is a small railroad based in the region it serves, it can offer its customers personalized service. And because it isn't burdened with a Class 1 railroad's high overhead, A&M can provide service at lower cost. The icing on the cake is that BN continues to receive much of the traffic generated by A&M. Some of the other railroads created in the wake of BN's program to trim its railroad map are Montana Rail Link, Washington Central, and the Kiamichi Railroad. BN also leases several hundred miles of

Some Frisco people worried that BN would chew up the Frisco — and their jobs — after the 1980 BN-Frisco merger.

track in South Dakota abandoned by the Milwaukee Road in the early 1980s and purchased by the state of South Dakota. BN moves its headquarters to Fort Worth.

SO WHERE DOES that leave the BN today? In two words, big and profitable. Big because even after spin-offs and abandonments of unprofitable branch lines,

BN remains the largest railroad in the U.S. with 29,000 route-miles. Its locomotive fleet is big too: 2,957 units. And profitable because 33 percent of BN's revenue comes from coal mined in the Powder River Basin region of Montana and Wyoming and hauled to power plants all over the U.S.

They used to call coal "black diamonds," and for good reason: You can't damage it, it moves in unit trains that don't require a lot of handling, and there's no danger of running out of the stuff in the next one hundred years or so. And because the coal BN hauls is low sulphur and burns cleaner than its high-sulphur counterpart it's in high demand. You could say that BN's future looks good and black.

There's always a chance that BN will merge with a large eastern railroad — Norfolk Southern, for example — and create the first true transcontinental railroad. If that day ever happens, I'm sure that somewhere on the new railroad an employee from one of the predecessor railroads will mutter, "This used to be a damned good railroad. But now it's all gone to hell."

BN stands at 29,000 route-miles, including the 40 miles track inspector Archie Shoto will ride between Chicago and Aurora, Ill.

PAUL D. SCHNEIDER PHOTO

CHAPTER 1

*Let the
locomotive
retirements begin*

RING OUT
THE OLD

I FOUND THE Burlington Northern's Alco FAs by accident. Over the 1972 Labor Day weekend I headed south from my home in Bellingham, Wash., to Vancouver, Wash., to look for the FAs that BN had recently retired. "They ain't here," said the BN shop foreman at Vancouver when I asked him the whereabouts of the FAs. "Been gone for a coupla weeks now, I think."

He had no idea where they'd gone — maybe to some junkyard in Portland, he suggested. If that was the case, I was out of luck. My trip had consisted mainly of talking my way aboard various BN freight trains to get to Vancouver to search for the FAs. Getting to Portland wasn't as simple as jumping in a car and driving Interstate 5 across the Columbia River and prowling around the city looking for junkyards. More importantly, I had to start making plans to work my way

The decline of passenger service on BN spelled troubled times for the future of E8A 9950 at Denver in 1970.

F. HOL WAGNER, JR. PHOTO

back north to Bellingham to get to work on Tuesday morning. Riding freights, I'd found, wasn't like riding a passenger train where you simply paid your fare, showed up at train time, and climbed aboard for the ride. If I couldn't get on a freight out of Vancouver for Seattle, or if I missed connecting with a Bellingham-bound freight out of Seattle, I'd be doomed to hitchhike back or something even more painful: shelling out what little cash I had to ride Amtrak, which in 1972 operated a daily Seattle-Vancouver, B.C. train via

Bellingham.

With these thoughts in mind I caught a ride with the first freight that departed Vancouver yard on Monday morning. Our power that day consisted of three high-horsepower units, the last an ex-Great Northern SD45 still wearing its original GN orange and green colors. It was a lovely late summer morning, perfect for the sunny-day color slide photography of locomotives that was my passion at the time, but frankly I couldn't have cared less. What good were clear skies when I couldn't

BN's Alco FAs bridged the world of freight service in the Pacific Northwest and passenger commuter service in New York.

find the FAs I'd spent the weekend looking for? I didn't even bother to shoot the SD45 in our train's power consist. SD45s were modern, state-of-the-art locomotives. After all, EMD was still building them new for other railroads. They'd be around forever.

My train wasn't exactly the *Pacific Zip*, at that time BN's premier train between Chicago and Seattle. We stopped at every major station along the 176-mile route between Vancouver and Seattle, setting out and picking up cars like a local. Not only had I not found the FAs, it looked like it would take me forever to get back to Bellingham.

Shortly after noon our train rolled into Tacoma, Wash., 40 miles south of Seattle. We rumbled past the Tacoma passenger depot, a domed monstrosity that had seen better days, and curved past a dilapidated roundhouse at the south end of a BN freight yard populated by the locomotives most common to this line at the time: Ex-Northern Pacific Geeps and switchers. As

if such mundane power wasn't bad enough, Tacoma smelled like someone had just passed gas, a stink that could be traced to the numerous paper mills we skirted along the Puget Sound waterfront. I figured the sooner I got out of Tacoma, the better.

Then my train rolled around the curve at the north end of the yard and I saw the FAs.

was slowing down as it approached an old wooden interlocking tower named "Reservation." Well, reservations were the last thing I had as I bailed off the train with a hurried wave to the head-end crew.

I walked over to the yard track and stared amazed at my elusive quarry. The FAs were coupled nose-to-nose, which meant that none of them had an unobstructed nose for what I considered the "ideal" locomotive roster shot. Somehow it didn't matter. I was in the presence of antiquity: These were some of the last FAs to operate in the U.S. What they were doing parked on a yard track in Tacoma didn't matter.

As I prowled around the cab of the middle unit I heard the clank of my train starting to pull out of Tacoma. I felt a tug of apprehension. After all, I was 140 miles from Bellingham, with little more than six or seven hours of daylight left. I had no idea if I'd make it back to Seattle in time to connect with the last BN freight to

Three of them sat in a row west of the main. I stared at them in disbelief. Somewhere in my brain an alarm bell sounded and told me to get off the train. I scrambled around gathering my gear. The train

Bellingham. As I pondered what to do, my train disappeared past Reservation tower on the last leg of its trip into Seattle.

How was I going to get home? I'd worry about that later. For now the world consisted of the BN's last FAs and me.

THE BN FAs I found in Tacoma that day were merely a fraction of the locomotives BN has retired since the March 3, 1970, merger. BN retires locomotives for much the same reasons most railroads retire locomotives: They are old, worn out, or technologically obsolete (and thus expensive to maintain and repair).

Take the FAs, for example. Their cab unit configuration rendered them obsolete in a world where the functional hood unit reigned almost unchallenged on road freights, locals, and branch lines. Historically the Alco 244 diesel engines that powered the FAs and their cousins on BN's roster, the RS2s and RS3s, had long been plagued by a poor crankshaft design that frequently led to crankcase explosions, a nasty and expensive problem to repair. In the last analysis the FAs — constructed for BN predecessor Spokane, Portland & Seattle in 1949 and 1950 — were simply worn out.

The obsolescence of the cab unit carbodies (often called "covered wagons") was also BN's motivation for retiring large numbers of F units, the FAs' EMD coun-

In 1978 BN lowered the boom on several of its aging Alco RS3s, including 4081 in a scrapyard in Tacoma, Wash.
PAUL D. SCHNEIDER PHOTO

BN's cab units weren't as practical as road-switchers, which is why this C&S SD9 outlived F7A 620.

F. HOL WAGNER, JR. PHOTO

terparts, even though the F's shared identical mechanical and electrical innards with their hood unit cousins, EMD's GP and SD road-switchers. It was much the same matter when it came to the F's six-axle counterpart, EMD's E units. BN's E's were built exclusively for passenger service, already a shrinking market when BN came into existence in 1970. Passenger service became even less important when Amtrak took over most U.S. intercity passenger trains a year later and slashed service by more than half. The sudden surplus of passenger diesels prompted BN to bump former passenger-service F units into freight service. But the E units were another story, one that ended with the retirement of all of BN's E7s and some E8s.

What usually happens to the locomotives BN retires? When I bade farewell to the BN's FAs and climbed aboard a northbound freight later that evening in 1972, I presumed the FAs would wind up scrapped and recycled into chain link fences. Not so. Although the units I found had indeed been sold to scrap dealer Joseph Simon & Sons of Tacoma, the dealer sold them to the Long Island Rail Road, which at that time was looking for second-hand Alco cab units to remanufacture into power cars for its push-pull commuter trains. Push-pull trains operate with the locomotive pushing the train one direction and pulling the train the other way. The problem is that push-pull trains require a locomotive equipped with head-end power (HEP) to provide electricity for the train, as well as a place for crews to ride when the locomotive is pushing at the other end. The power cars that Long Island converted

use the FAs' original engine (down-rated from 1,500 to 600 h.p.) to run an HEP generator that provides HEP. As icing on the cake, the power cars (which are known as "power packs") provide a place for the head-end crew to ride when the train is being pushed. Twenty years after I'd walked away from the FAs I found in Tacoma in 1972, I stood on a parking

Details such as these on the side of a former GN passenger F-unit (above) vanished along with these ex-GN and ex-NP Fs (left) at Denver's 7th Street shop.

PAUL D. SCHNEIDER TOP PHOTO
F. HOL WAGNER, JR. LEFT PHOTO

21

garage roof in Mineola, N.Y., and watched one of those same units leading a commuter train from New York up the Oyster Bay branch line as an EMD GP38-2 pushed on the rear. Granted, this isn't exactly the service that God and Alco had intended for the FAs when they were built in 1949. Still, the FAs survive in some form, a fate that doesn't always await a retired BN unit.

Take, for example, BN's first 704, an F3 cab unit. Upon retirement in April 1970, this ex-NP unit was shuffled off to EMD as a trade-in credit on BN SD45s 6472-6497. Like trading in your old car on a new one, locomotive trade-ins are a way for a railroad to reduce the price of a new locomotive. Unlike your trade-in, though, the units are unlikely to end up on a used-locomotive lot with "low miles" or "super saver" soaped on their windshields. Before the 1970s, a railroad might have asked the builder to recycle certain components in the new locomotive. Great Northern,

Who would have thought that BN's only Alco S6 (below) would be rebuilt by Morrison-Knudsen as a road slug (right) for log-hauler Columbia & Cowlitz in Longview, Wash.

PAUL C. HUNNELL BOTTOM PHOTO
J. DAVID INGLES COLLECTION
PAUL D. SCHNEIDER RIGHT PHOTO

for example, purchased EMD GP9s with some electrical components recycled from traded-in FT cab units (the new units, dubbed "GP5s," became BN 1350-1365). Most of the time, though, trade-in units are simply resold to a scrap dealer, which often strips them for resale components and scraps the hulks.

Finally there are those retired BN units that are dealt what may be the luckiest card of all. They are sold for service — not scrap — to another party, either a rail-

NRL is a contract locomotive shop in Dixmoor, Ill., that leases retired BN F45s such as this (right) to power-short railroads. BN gave the heave-ho to its SD24s in 1981, but two units (below) found a home on shortline Fox River Valley R.R. in Wisconsin.

PAUL D. SCHNEIDER PHOTOS

road, a locomotive dealer, or an industrial customer. Take BN NW2 586, for example. It was born in April 1948 as No. 115 of the New York, Ontario & Western Railway, a struggling 541-mile road from Cornwell, N.Y., to Scranton, Pa., and Oswego, N.Y. When NYO&W gave up the ghost in 1957, No. 115 was auctioned off to BN predecessor Northern Pacific, which christened it 99. After the BN merger, NP 99 became BN 586, the number it carried until it was sold in August 1982 to locomotive dealer Hyman-Michaels Co. At that point it seemed as if the 34-year-old unit

would follow the path of the NYO&W into railroad history. Instead, Hyman-Michaels resold 586 in 1986 to Cargill Grain Co., which didn't even bother to renumber the unit before assigning it to its Minot, N.D., facility.

Scrap, trade-in, or resale. There didn't seem to be much chance that BN's old and obsolete units would face anything other than one of these fates. But then, these locomotives had no idea what lay in store for them after 1974.

There's no mistaking the former identity of Indiana Hi-Rail Corp.'s Alco C424 at Henderson, Ky., in 1991.

PAUL D. SCHNEIDER PHOTO

CHAPTER 2

*BN's rolling
locomotive
museum*

A STAY
OF
EXECUTION

THE STATE OF THE BN'S locomotive retirements in the mid-1970s was never as clear to me as it was one day in April 1977. I lived in Wishram, Wash., at the time, working as an extra-board train-order operator on BN's Portland Division. One morning Andy Anderson, a former Spokane, Portland & Seattle man who'd recently retired as a BN locomotive engineer, knocked on the door of my two-room shack and told me to come to the engine terminal to see the old covered wagon.

The covered wagon turned out to be F9 cab unit 828, one of a group of freight F9s

Two BN Century-series Alcos stand tall at Wishram, Wash., in 1976— four years before their demise.

PAUL D. SCHNEIDER PHOTO

26

inherited from the Northern Pacific. Anderson poked at the unit as if he'd stumbled across a mummified dinosaur. "I haven't seen one of these in years," he said, peering at the spot where the builder's plate used to be.

To be sure, EMD F's were fast becoming a rarity on western Class 1 railroads. Union Pacific and Southern Pacific, for example, had long since gotten rid of their F's. And Santa Fe in the 1970s was transmogrifying its F units into road-switcher units (which it dubbed "CF7s" for Converted F7s).

The 828 at Wishram was, in fact, a symptom of an ailment BN suffered in the mid-1970s: a power shortage brought on by a surge in low-sulphur coal traffic out of Wyoming and Montana. Although BN was buying new six-motor 3,000 h.p. EMD SD40-2s and GE U30Cs and C30-7s as fast as the builders could crank them out, the demand for new power to meet the growth in coal traffic precluded trading in older, obsolete units as BN had done with F3A 704 back in 1970. On BN's Seattle-Portland Region, this meant that locomotives BN would have ordinarily dispatched to the happy hunting grounds — Alco RS3s and RS11s and EMD F's, GP7s, and NW5s — remained in service, thumbing their noses at the scrappers. As the new high-horsepower units marched into the coalfields to haul BN's profitable coal

An eye-popping variety of paint schemes and locomotive types characterized BN's locomotive fleet in the early 1970s.

EMD 7095 was one of hundreds of SD40-2s that BN bought in the mid-1970s to handle a boom in coal traffic in the Powder River Basin.

PAUL D. SCHNEIDER PHOTO

The Powder River Basin is where most of BN's GE C30-7s spent the 1970s hauling unit trains of low-sulphur coal.

trains, a new operating philosophy went into effect with the locomotives left to haul secondary and other lower-priority freights elsewhere on the system: If it had a working headlight and smoke coming out of its stack, stick it on the point of a train and keep your fingers crossed.

Nor were such locomotives limited to secondary and local trains. Train No. 23, BN's westbound intermodal train between Spokane and Portland via Wishram, normally rated two or three six-motor high-horsepower units (often 3,600 h.p. Alco C636s). But in March 1977 I stood in front

of the depot at Roosevelt, Wash., a train order station 40 miles east of Wishram, and watched in amazement as No. 23 stormed through town behind some of the last road locomotives I'd ever expected to see on the point of a hot train on a Class 1 railroad: a pair of 1,600 h.p. Alco RS3s built in 1955.

It was much the same story on the Chicago Region, to which I transferred in January 1979 as an extra board operator working out of Aurora, Ill., on BN's Chicago-Aurora main line. There I witnessed the same stay of execution for

NW2s and SW1s in switch service, GP7s and SD7s in local and transfer service, and GP20s, SD24s, U25Bs, and U28Bs in through freight service. Like the F's and Alcos in the Pacific Northwest, the old EMDs and GEs assigned to the Chicago Region were holding down BN's motive power fort until fresh troops rode to the rescue.

THE EASING of BN's motive power crunch had as much to do with outside economic forces as it did with the arrival of new locomotives in the coalfields. In late 1979 the economy started to falter,

After a recession flattened traffic in 1980, BN used SD40-2s like this trio in Montana (top) to bump off many older obsolete diesels. Older six-motor GEs gave way to SD40-2s on the coal trains delivered to Minnesota Power & Light's Cohasset power plant (left).

MIKE DANNEMAN TOP PHOTO
PAUL D. SCHNEIDER BOTTOM PHOTO

Alco's C636 used
four fewer cylinders
to produce the same
3,600 h.p. as EMD's
20-cylinder SD45,
but that didn't save
BN's 10 C636s
from retirement in
1980.

and by 1980 the U.S. was floundering in a recession that flattened railroad traffic levels.

For BN, the recession was like the old joke about good news and bad news. The bad news was that because of the slow economy, the railroad was running fewer and shorter trains. The good news was that the drop in tonnage meant BN needed fewer locomotives to operate its trains. With enough reliable power to operate both its merchandise and coal trains, BN heaved a sigh of relief, canceled an order for new SD40-2s and C30-7s, and went back to sweeping old and obsolete locomotives off the property.

The first units to go were the Alcos. The fact that Alco Products had gone out of business in 1969 meant that BN's Alcos

Century-series Alcos (top) held down BN's motive-power fort in the Pacific Northwest until EMD replacements arrived in 1980. The C636 (left) leading train 139 across the Columbia River near Wishram, Wash., in 1978 is only a few years away from being scrapped by Chrome Locomotive.

PAUL D. SCHNEIDER TOP PHOTO
BLAIR KOOISTRA BOTTOM PHOTO

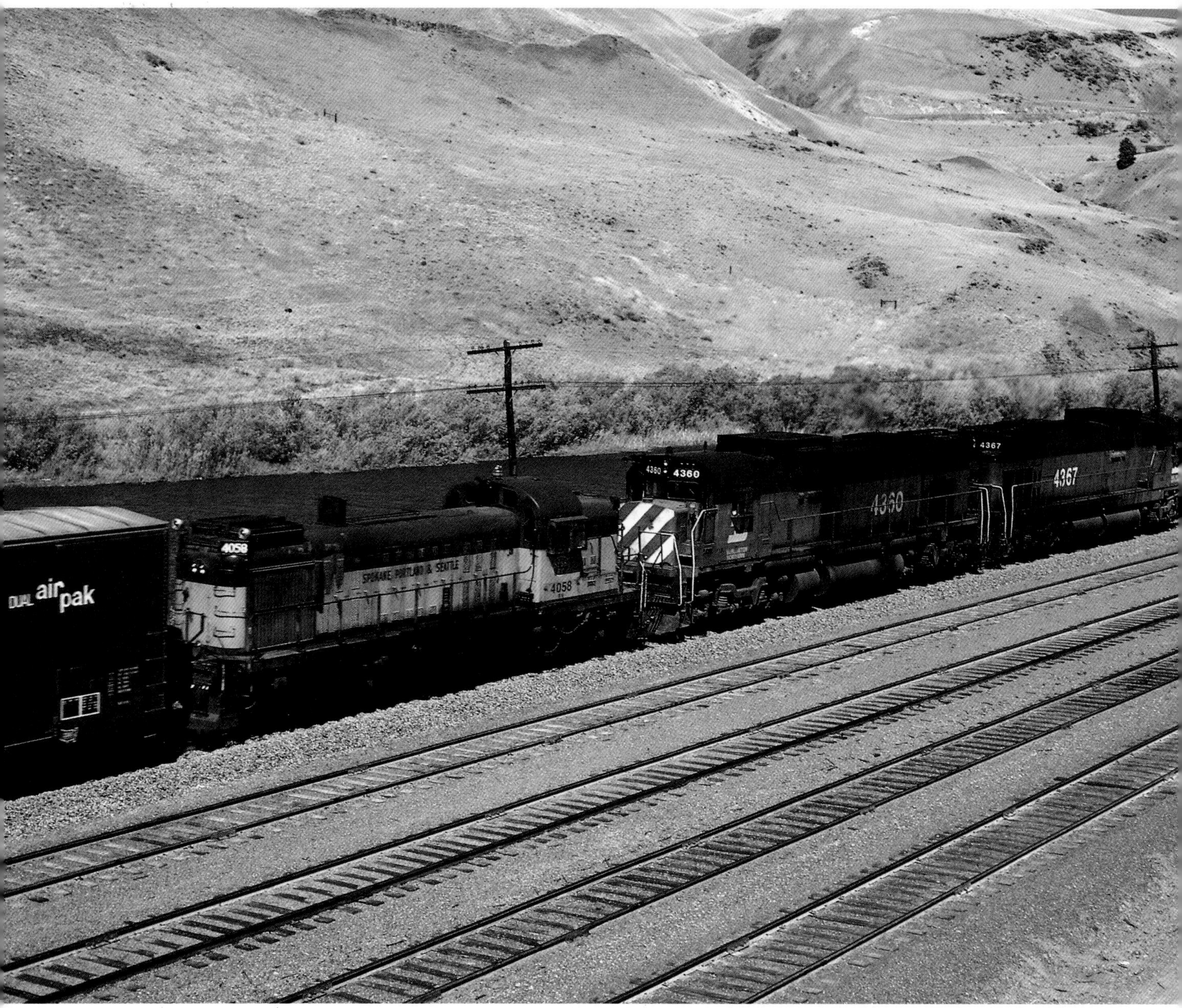

RS3 4058 (above) exchanged its SP&S colors for BN green in 1977, only to be sold for scrap a year later. One of the last locomotives (right) the author expected to see on a hot train on a Class One railroad: an Alco RS3 like BN 4064.

PAUL D. SCHNEIDER PHOTOS

were orphans in an EMD and GE world. Nor did it help that the 10 C636s and two C415s were equipped with Alco's "Hi-Ad" (high-adhesion) trucks, a unique design that proved troublesome. BN bundled all of its Alcos into deadlines in the Pacific Northwest just in time for the 1980 explosion of Mount St. Helens. Ironically, both C415s were sold, as were many of the 251-powered RS11s and four-motor Century-series road-switchers. Even a number of

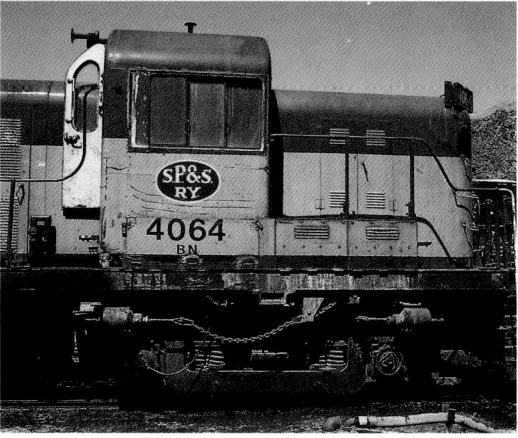

RS3s with their infamous 244 diesel engines were ultimately sold for service. And while most of the C636s met their fate at the scrapper's hand (demand among shortlines and industrial railroads being limited for high-horsepower, six-motor units riding on unpopular trucks), at least one unit was sold for service to Cliffs Western Australia Mining, an iron-ore hauler "down under."

Next to go were the 5600-series GE U25Cs and U28Cs. They had spent most of the 1970s toiling in the western coalfields, an appropriate place for a group of locomotives that shared many characteristics (six-powered axles, high horsepow-

Clean BN paint (above) didn't help the reliability of BN's aging Alco RS3s and RS11s, but hey, at least they looked good. Chrome Crankshaft in Chicago spruced up several ex-BN Alcos (left) for Kyle Railroad in Kansas.

PAUL D. SCHNEIDER PHOTOS

By 1980 BN considered its oldest U-series GEs to be obsolete, including these 25Cs and U28Cs stored unserviceable at Cicero, Ill., (this page) and U25B's such as 5411 in GN paint at Galesburg, Ill., (top right). U25Cs like 5621 at Alliance, Neb., (bottom right) bore the brunt of western coal train service until they were replaced by new locomotives in 1981.

er) with the SD40-2s and C30-7s that replaced them.

Two things doomed the 5600s. One was that they had aged hard and fast in one of the most demanding types of train service: lugging heavy unit coal trains. Second was what motive power officials politely refer to as "obsolete technology."

J. DAVID INGLES COLLECTION TOP PHOTO
F. HOL WAGNER, JR. BOTTOM PHOTO

Frisco's red-and-white paint scheme didn't save its U25Bs from kicking the bucket with their ex-Burlington and ex-GN brethren.

PAUL D. SCHNEIDER PHOTO

When they were built, the 5600s (and their four-motor sister GE U25Bs and U28Bs) were state-of-the-art locomotives. But by 1980, their '60s-era technology had been surpassed by such improvements as GE's own Dash 7 electrical wizardry, improved traction motors, and all the other features GE sales representatives used to persuade railroads to trade in their old GEs on new Dash 7s. For most of the 1970s BN couldn't afford to spare the 5600s as trade-in fodder. But in the depths of the 1980 recession, that was no longer an issue, and the 5600s were sold for scrap in 1981. BN's 5400-series U25Bs and U28Bs kicked the bucket and were sold for scrap the following year.

Electro Motive diesels weren't immune from retirement's kiss of death. GP7 1587 rolling past Aurora tower in Aurora, Ill., (top) was vanquished with all of BN's 567B-powered road switchers. BN's SD24s may have helped usher in dieseldom's "second generation" in 1959, but by 1982 they were on the brink of extinction.

PAUL D. SCHNEIDER TOP PHOTO
J. DAVID INGLES BOTTOM PHOTO

If BN's older EMD products chuckled over the fate of the railroads' Alcos and older GEs, they had little to laugh about by 1982 when BN side-tracked its ex-Burlington EMD SD24s. The SD24 was part of a motive power era that *Trains* editor David P. Morgan dubbed the "second generation" of diesels. The 1959 debut of GE's ground-breaking 2,500 h.p. U25B sparked a locomotive revolution characterized by a heightened interest in high-horsepower locomotives with six-motor trucks for high-speed freight service. By

the 1980s that second generation had reached middle age, and the 567-engined SD24 had long been superseded by EMD's state-of-the-art six-motor, high-horsepower unit, the SD40-2. Like BN's older GEs, the SD24s were technologically obsolete, the main reason BN retired them in 1982 (and a good reason as of 1991 only four non-remanufactured SD24s survive out of the 179 built).

THE EXODUS of F units that had been going on since the early years of the 1970

merger became a covered-wagon cattle drive in the early 1980s. BN's decision to give the boot to the last of its 567B-engined F3s and F7s was part of a plan to simplify the railroad's EMD 567 parts inventory by retaining only those units powered by the newer 567C-series engine. The purge that ensued included all of BN's NW2 switchers, which were built with 567 and 567A type engines; all but one of the similarly equipped 600 h.p. SW1s; and all 567B-powered NW5s, GP7s, and SD7s.

There were, however, two notable ex-

ceptions to BN's "EMD 567C members only" locomotive club. Included in the club were BN's 567A-powered SW7s and 567B-powered SW9s, most of which didn't start to disappear until the mid-1980s. Their stay of execution was granted by the high cost of new replacement switchers, money which BN preferred to spend on new road units such as GE B30-7As and EMD GP50s. On the other hand, the 700- and 800-series F9 cabs — which were powered by 567C engines — were excluded from the club, mainly because their cab-unit configuration rendered them as impractical as the BN FAs and early EMD F's that had preceded them into retirement. Nonetheless, several of the F9s managed to cheat the grim reaper, which is more than can be said about many of the units that were retired after 1982.

One of the NW2s owned by BN subsidiary Lake Superior Terminal & Transportation (opposite page) wound up switching for Cargill Grain in Dubuque, Ia. Never mind the marker lights on 470 (left) or the years that 543 (below) spent switching suburban coaches in Chicago— both units were tossed off by BN in 1983.

PAUL D. SCHNEIDER PHOTOS

CHAPTER 3

*Off to that
big roundhouse
in the sky*

DON'T
FEAR
THE REAPER

BETWEEN 1983 AND 1987 the faces of the locomotives BN retired changed, but the song remained the same. In no particular order, BN gave the heave-ho to a large number of second-generation units: all SD45s, SDP45s, F45s; a significant number of GP20s, SD40s, and SDP40s from builder Electro-Motive; most U23Cs, U33Cs, U28Bs, and U30Bs; and some U30Cs from General Electric. Historically these locomotives had superseded dieseldom's "first generation" of covered wagons and early road-switchers. But the triumph of these second-generation

It looks like BN on the outside, but F45 6642 is one of National Railway Equipment's lease-locomotives.
PAUL D. SCHNEIDER PHOTO

44

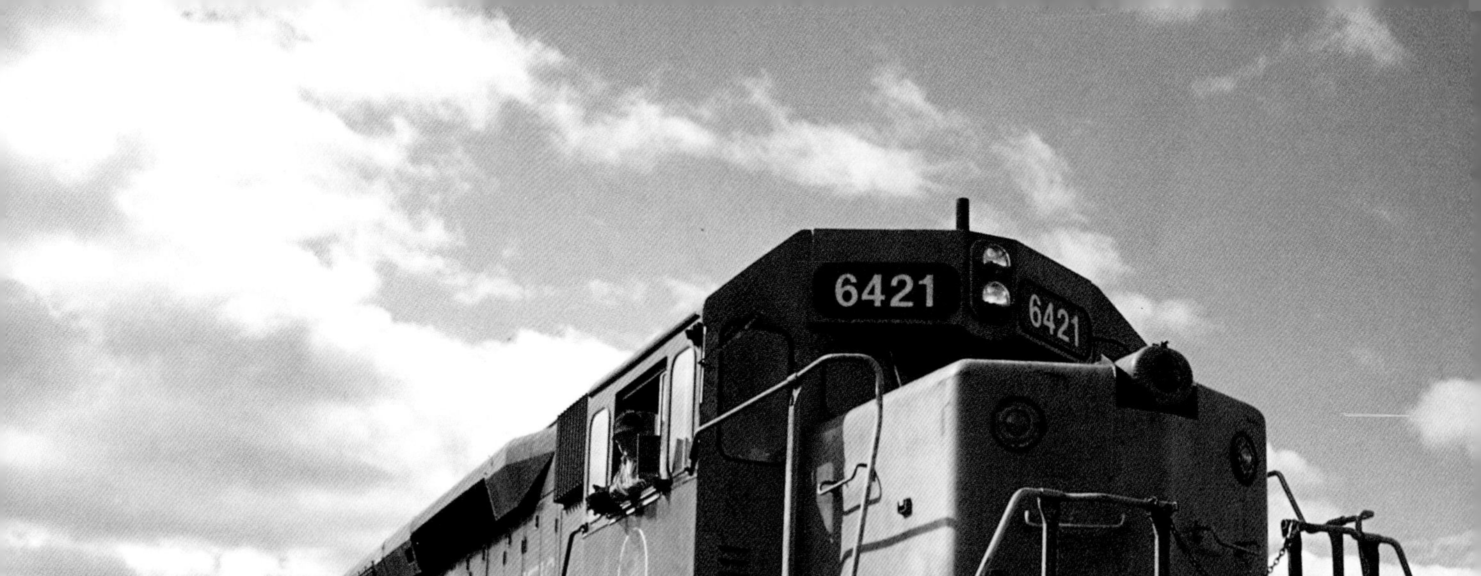

Two BN predecessors that used SD45s on their mainline freights were NP (top) and GN (bottom).

PAUL D. SCHNEIDER TOP PHOTO

JOHN STUBBLEFIELD BOTTOM PHOTO J. DAVID INGLES COLLECTION

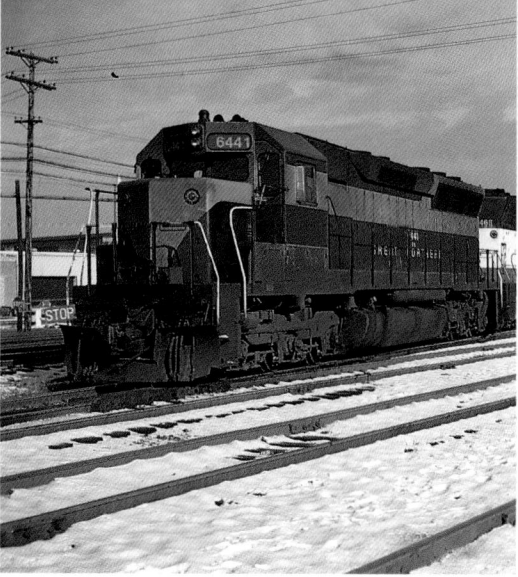

locomotives had long since faded, leaving them prey to the same maladies — age, technological obsolescence, high mileage, and high maintenance cost — as the locomotives they had replaced.

Many of these high-horsepower units were financed by banks and other financial institutions, which then leased the units to BN for 15 years. When the lease expired, BN simply turned the units back to the lessors. The returned units were then sold, often for reuse by other railroads. In 1989, for example, BN turned back 11 U30Cs to the lessor, which in turn resold five for service to Upper Michigan iron-ore hauler Lake Superior & Ishpeming.

By far the lion's share of high-horsepower units resold for service were BN's big 20-cylinder EMD SD45s, F45s, and SDP45s. Several months before BN merged with the St. Louis-San Francisco (Frisco) on November 21, 1980, a shop

New SD45s delivered to BN included 6553 (bottom) rolling through North Dakota and 6497 (top) which was ordered by CB&Q prior to the merger.

PAUL D. SCHNEIDER PHOTOS

The F45 features
a full-width cab
(above). 6627 went
from BN (right)
to an excursion train
operator, then short-
line Wisconsin and
Southern.

PAUL D. SCHNEIDER TOP PHOTO
BRUCE KELLY RIGHT PHOTO

foreman at Frisco's Springfield (Mo.) shop told me that his people referred to Frisco's SD45s as "whips" because of the long crankshaft in the 645E3 engine. "They act like whips when they break," he explained, "which happens a lot with these big 20-cylinder engines." To top it off, the SD45s were fuel hogs, hardly surprising considering that it took 20 cylinders to crank out 3,600 h.p. (compared with 16 cylinders in Alco's 3,600 h.p. C636 and GE's 3,300 h.p. U33Cs).

Not that the liabilities of the 20-cylinder engine seemed to bother the buyers that acquired many of BN's used SD45s, SDP45s, and F45s. Locomotive leasing firms such as Helm Leasing (identified as HLC on the side of unrepainted BN units), National Railway Leasing (NRL), and railroads such as New York, Susquehanna & Western, Montana Rail Link, and Wisconsin Central cherry-picked the best of BN's 225 20-cylinder EMDs. Wisconsin Central, in fact, embraced BN's SD45 to the tune of 40 units, most of which remain in service in 1991, whip crankshafts and all.

BY THE TIME the 1990s rolled around, a curious thing happened to BN locomotive retirements: They stopped.

Well, not entirely. Most of BN's tired

Frisco 938 and 45 sister SD45s were renumbered into the same 6600 number series as BN's F45s.

PAUL D. SCHNEIDER PHOTO

U30Cs had breathed their last by 1992, although a handful were still alive and kicking on January 1, 1993. And a number of wrecked units were stricken from the roster after the railroad deemed it economically unfeasible to repair them. But locomotives that were fast disappearing on other railroads—EMD GP9s and SD9s and higher-horsepower GP30s, GP35s, and GP40s — managed to avoid the kiss of death.

What happened was that BN decided to remanufacture many of its older, technologically obsolete EMD locomotives. The details of BN's "Competitive Remanu- facturing Program" can be found in Chap-

6655 marks WC's one-year anniversary (below). WC 6533 (right) once called BN's Interbay shop in Seattle home.

PAUL D. SCHNEIDER PHOTOS

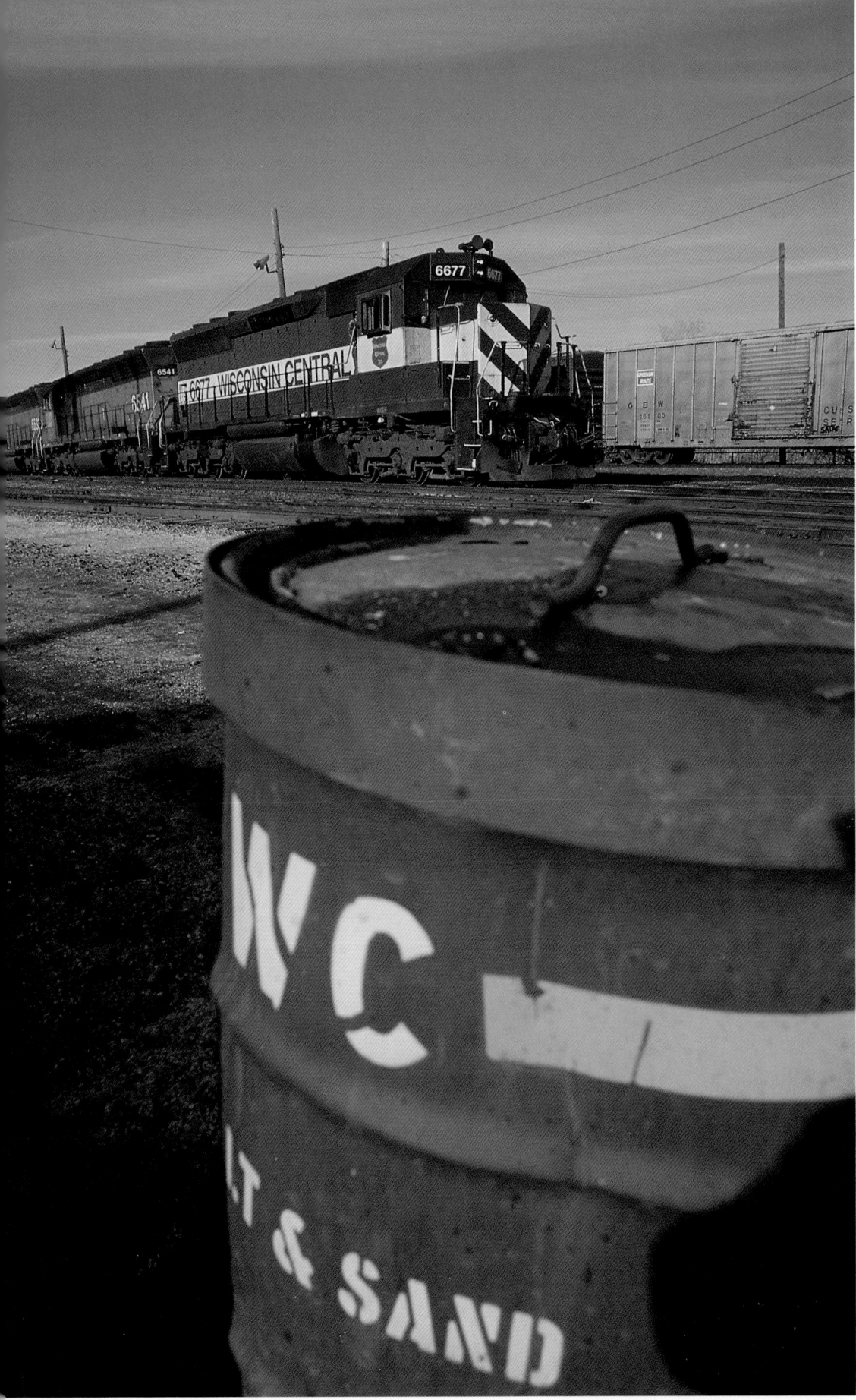

Regional railraod Wisconsin Central isn't inclined to can its 40 ex-BN SD45s.

PAUL D. SCHNEIDER PHOTO

C&NW re-sold some of its ex-BN SD45s (right) to VMV Enterprises. New York, Susquehanna & Western chose ex-BN SD45s and F45s (below) to haul its main line trains.

PAUL D. SCHNEIDER TOP PHOTO
SCOTT HARTLEY BOTTOM PHOTO

ter 5, but suffice it to say that most of the GP9s and second-generation EMDs were packed off to contract rebuilders for remanufacturing into what are almost new units.

The SD9s have a slightly different story. BN's need for efficient yard and transfer locomotives prompted the railroad in 1992 to send 11 aging SD9s off to VMV Enterprises of Paducah, Ky., for rebuilding into yard slugs. A yard slug is a weighted rail vehicle (often just an old locomotive hulk) with traction motors but no power source of its own. Instead it is coupled to a parent unit that supplies power to the slug's traction motors, a combination that provides extra tractive effort at a lower cost than two powered units.

Three ex-BN F45s on Wisconsin & Southern thumb their striped noses at retirement.

MIKE DANNEMAN PHOTO

53

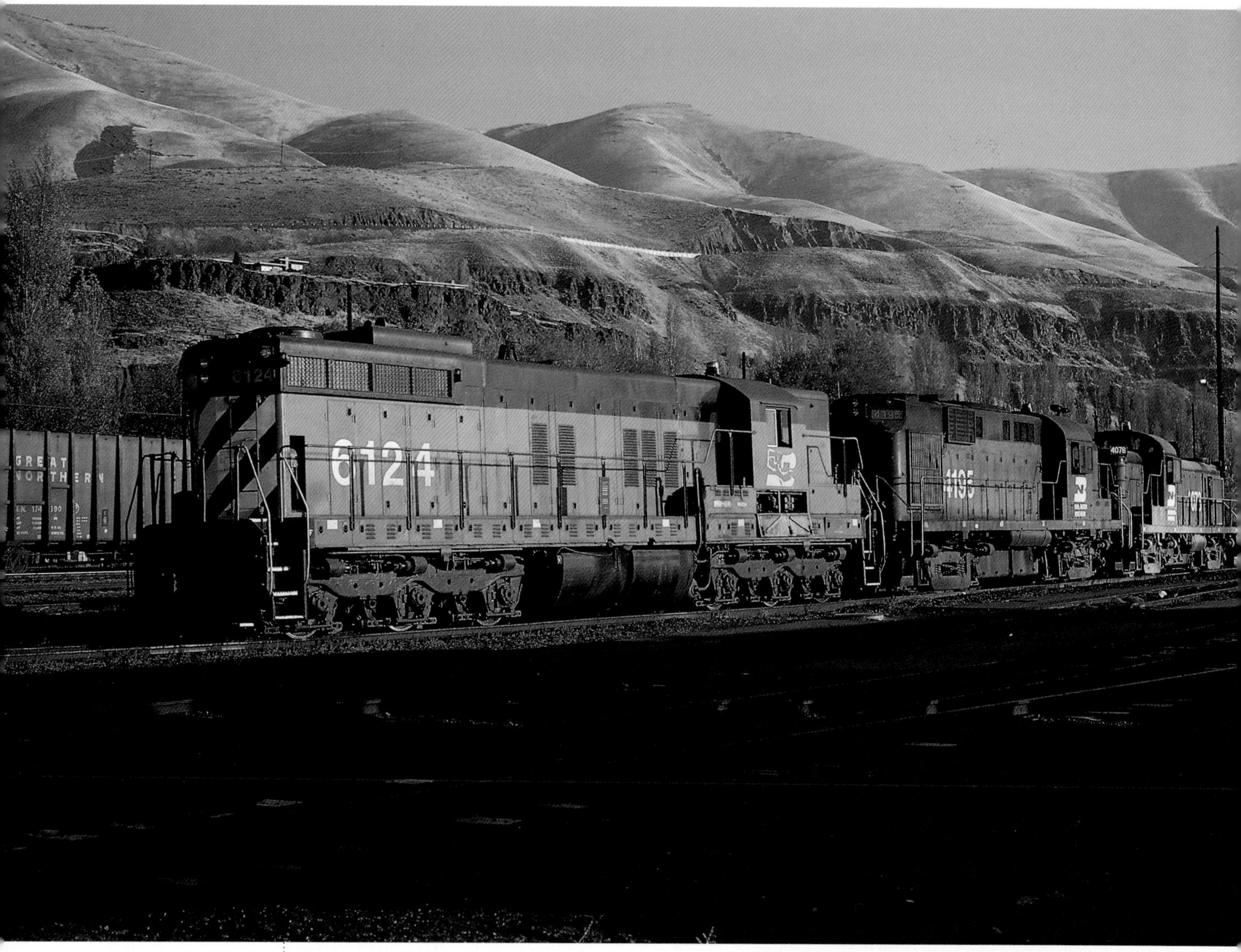

Despite their age, many BN SD9s (above and right) have outlasted the Alcos they once locked couplers with.

PAUL D. SCHNEIDER TOP PHOTO
OTTO P. DOBNICK RIGHT PHOTO

Although slugs come in both road and yard versions, BN asked VMV for a yard slug for low-speed switching and transfer work.

A transfer train operates between two connecting railroads in different parts of a switching district or urban area. In Chicago, for example, BN transfers double-stack traffic to Norfolk Southern. The double-stack trains arrive from the west and terminate at BN's Cicero Yard just west of downtown Chicago. A BN transfer train powered by a pair of SW1000s or SD9s then hauls the double stacks across Chicago to Norfolk Southern's Calumet

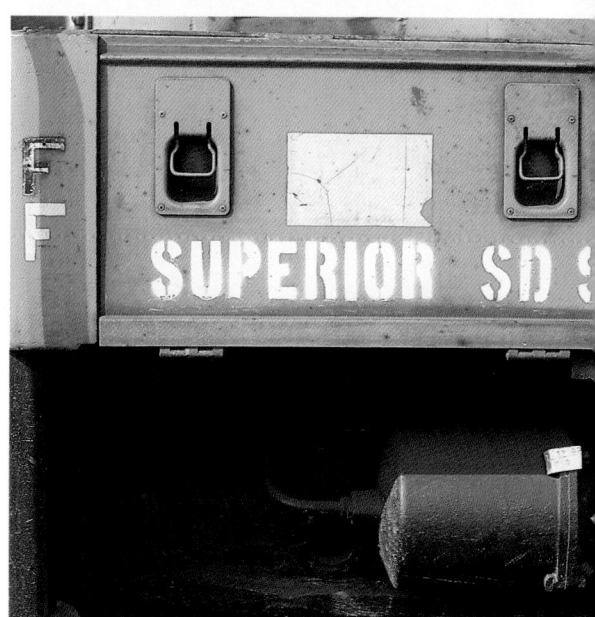

Yard. After the transfer delivers the double-stack cars to NS, the locomotives head back to Cicero Yard, sometimes with a transfer from NS in tow.

What VMV produced for BN is a yard slug with a twist: an operator's cab with desktop controls that allow a crew member to operate the parent-slug set from the slug itself. The resulting TEBC6 looks like a cartoon version of a switch engine with a ve-e-e-ry long carbody mounted on a pair of EMD six-motor Flexicoil trucks. The idea is that the crew on a yard-transfer job can ride facing forward regardless of which direction the parent locomotive is facing. In this case, the parent locomotives are BN's four SD38-2s (6260-6263) and seven additional units supplied by VMV, a mix of former Norfolk Southern and CSXT SD35s that have been rebuilt

A transfer train (above) powered by SW1000 384 rolls through Chicago in September 1990. BN reassigned SD9s (left) from secondary trains like this one in Colorado to big-city transfers.

PAUL D. SCHNEIDER TOP PHOTO
F. HOL WAGNER, JR. LEFT PHOTO

to what BN and VMV call "SD38-2Ps." The name springs from the fact that the original 2,500 h.p. 567 diesel engines in the VMV-supplied SD35s have been upgraded with 2,000 h.p. 645 power assemblies and Dash 2 electricals, the same specs as an EMD SD38-2. The "P" stands for "parent" unit, the politically correct term for what used to be a "master" unit (which controlled a "slave").

The TEBC6s are a sign that the rules of the locomotive retirement game are changing. Sure, it was still possible in 1993 to find a BN SD9 rusting away in a scrapyard in McCook, Ill., waiting to meet its fate at the scrapper's torch. But many of BN's other SD9s may likely end up surviving, albeit in a highly modified form, as slugs. And BN has hinted that the SD9s

Look what they've done to my SD9, ma! New TEBC6s pose at VMV's shop (opposite page) and Chicago (bottom).

LON COONE LEFT PHOTO
PAUL A. BERGEN COLLECTION
PAUL D. SCHNEIDER BOTTOM PHOTO

PAUL D. SCHNEIDER PHOTO

themselves may wind up as parent units someday. If and when that happens, the SD9s will avoid the unhappy fate of the F3s, C424s, U30Cs, and hundreds of other retired units that BN has retired since 1970.

58

EMD leased BN
6340 to Soo in 1988
with just a GM nose
logo (left). In 1992 it
wore EMD colors
(opposite page)
to promote EMD's
after-market prod-
ucts. Illinois Central
(below) picked up
the lease on a
group of retired BN
SD40-2s in 1992.

G. ALLBACH LEFT PHOTO
PAUL A. BERGEN COLLECTION
SCOTT HARTLEY BOTTOM PHOTO

*Innovations
in high-horsepower
locomotives*

BIG BOMBERS

I KNEW A YARDMASTER who in 1979 referred to BN's high-horsepower six-axle diesels as "big bombers." It struck me as an appropriate nickname for the locomotives at the top of BN's motive power hierarchy at the time: 3,600 h.p. Alco C636s, 3,600 h.p. EMD SD45s, and 3,300 h.p. GE U33Cs.

Big bombers is also an appropriate nickname for locomotives such as the 3,800 h.p. Oakway SD60Ms and 3,900 h.p. LMX B39-8s that power many BN road freights. But these and the other high-horsepower units that BN fields in the 1990s are a far cry from their 1970s predecessors. We're not just talking about a new model designation in the shop manual and a different number series, folks. We're talking *different*.

Consider those Oakway SD60Ms and LMX B39-8s. Before they arrived on BN rails the railroad's acquisition of new power was a

New SD60M 9210 is a shining example of BN's high-horse-power six-axle "big bombers."

PAUL D. SCHNEIDER PHOTO

BN cab unit No. 1 stares down Oakway 9055 at the Electro-Northern shop in North Kansas City.

PAUL D. SCHNEIDER PHOTO

relatively simple matter. New models from EMD and GE were acquired under long-term equipment leases (15 years was the norm) arranged through banks and other financial institutions.

In an attempt to reduce the cost of acquiring new locomotives, BN in 1986 introduced a concept known as "power by the hour." Banks, investors, and other financial institutions purchased new locomotives (100 EMD SD60s and 100 GE B39-8s) and lease them to third-party companies (Oakway and LMX, respectively). BN buys only the electric power gener-

ated by the locomotives. The advantages are that EMD and GE have a direct economic interest in the performance of their units because the third-party companies contract with both builders to secure specific, long-term maintenance and performance-standard commitments. The agreements also include incentives if specific performance levels are met and penalties if they're not. Thus the builders have a reason to design and build units that are more reliable, less costly to maintain, and perform more consistently.

Numbers spell the success of the

"power by the hour" concept. For years BN struggled to achieve a 92-day maintenance cycle, the length of time that the Federal Railroad Administration allows a locomotive to operate between shop inspections. In 1986, for example, BN's 3100-series EMD GP50s averaged 31 to 35 days between major locomotive failures, not exactly something to write home about. But BN's power-by-the-hour units average 85 to 95 days of service between failures that require a shop visit. The result: The locomotive spends more time on the road making money for BN hauling freight instead of sitting around waiting

The Oakways wear EMD colors, but they're owned by investors who lease them to Oakway (left). Regardless of the number of units on a train (above) BN buys only the electricity the Oakways generate.

STEVE PATTERSON TOP PHOTO
PAUL D. SCHNEIDER BOTTOM PHOTO

Oakways roll a double-stack train through Devil's Canyon in Washington in 1987 (right). BN buys electricity from locomotives supplied by both Oakway and LMX (below).

to have a power assembly or traction motor replaced.

The 100 Oakway units are maintained by EMD at Electro Northern, a joint undertaking involving BN, EMD, and several shopcraft unions. EMD has a long-term lease on the Electro Northern shop, located next to BN's locomotive service area at Murray Yard in North Kansas City, Mo.

BN isn't the only winner with power by the hour. EMD doesn't have the resources to saturate the field with service people. Therefore the longer a particular locomotive model is in service, the less EMD learns about it over time. But Electro Northern provides a direct link to EMD.

A BN person with a problem has to wade through BN's organizational hierarchy, and the problem stands a chance of being downplayed or forgotten. But the manager of locomotive maintenance at Electro Northern simply picks up the telephone and calls General Motors Locomotive Group (GMLG) to deal quickly with a problem. In this way Electro Northern provides EMD with plenty of feedback on the performance of the SD60s. In the final analysis, it's a win-win situation for BN *and* GMLG.

THE OAKWAY SD60s weren't BN's first encounter with EMD's SD60 model. The first units were three units leased for demonstration purposes in November 1985. They were numbered BN 8300-8302

The Oakways on this coal train at Kansas City are one of several flavors of SD60s that BN has sampled since 1987.

PAUL D. SCHNEIDER PHOTO

5497 (below) was one of three GE B32-8s that BN tested before it acquired 100 LMX B39-8s.

PAUL D. SCHNEIDER TOP PHOTO
BILL FOLSOM BOTTOM PHOTO

and wore BN's "tiger-stripe" paint scheme like the 3100-series GP50s. At the end of their lease in November 1987 the three demonstrators were returned to EMD, where they joined EMD's fleet of leased locomotives, still wearing BN paint but with all Burlington Northern identification painted out.

The 100 9200-series SD60Ms that followed the Oakway SD60s in 1989 were built in London, Ontario, by General Motors Locomotive Group (which includes EMD, the former parent company). The units have GMLG's "super cab" for increased crew protection and comfort. The first 50 had three-piece cab windshields, while the remainder of the group came with two-piece windshields. As if to underscore the difference, the white paint applied to the cabs of the first order differed considerably from that applied to the units in the second order. Neither variation looks particularly suited to the

contours of the SD60M cab, but BN claims that the white paint on the cab face serves a purpose: to increase visibility of the units, thereby reducing the possibility of grade-crossing accidents.

The BN paint on the SD60Ms (regardless of the differences in their paint) underscores the fact that this version of the SD60 is not power by the hour. According to BN, the power by the hour concept upset many of the traditional ways of doing leveraged locomotive leasing. Some financial people normally involved with equipment leasing got cold feet when asked to become involved with the concept because power by the hour, to quote one BN official, "was a different animal that required a lot of lawyer time."

Although the 9200-series SD60Ms are not power by the hour, they do have something in common with their Oakway counterparts: The builder, not BN, is responsi-

LMX 8535 shares BN's Cicero, Ill., terminal with Oakway and BN SD60s in 1991 (below). A crew member lends a human touch to the high-tech cab of LMX 8563 (left).
PAUL D. SCHNEIDER PHOTOS

The LMXs on this train on Crawford Hill in Nebraska wear builder General Electric's colors.

MIKE DANNEMAN PHOTO

ble for their maintenance. The 9200s are maintained under a "shared facility" concept first used by GE to maintain the LMX B39-8s at BN's Lincoln (Neb.) shop. Under the 17- to 20-year agreement, the 9200s are maintained at BN's Glendive (Mont.) shop by BN employees working under the direction of EMD management technicians. Electro-Motive prescribes the scope, methodology, priorities, and standards of the SD60M maintenance and determines the number of BN people required to perform the work. Those people remain BN employees working under the applicable labor contracts, receiving BN paychecks, and covered by all regular

To promote grade-crossing visibility, the red logo on the side of the LMX units (left) was applied to the nose of units such as 8583 (above) at Cicero, Ill.

PAUL D. SCHNEIDER PHOTOS

69

railroad benefits. The BN shop superin-tendent is responsible for coordinating the joint operations.

PERHAPS THE most intriguing of BN's SD60s are its four 9500-series SD60 MACs. One of the key differences between these units and earlier SD60s is the SD60MAC's HTCR trucks. Since the intro-duction of the Dash 2 locomotive line in 1972, most EMD six-motor locomotives have ridden on HT-C trucks. "HT" stands for "high traction," and "C" means a three-axle, three-motor truck.

The "R" in HTCR stands for "radial," which means that the axles orient them-selves to the curvature of the track. GMLG calls what the HTCR truck does "self-regulated axle steering," a phrase often shortened to simply "self-steering." Regard-less of what you call them, the HTCR trucks provide greater adhesion in curves, lower wheel and rail wear, less locomotive maintenance, and extended intervals between overhaul, all of which mean less cost to BN. These trucks, incidentally, trace their origins to the HTBB truck that EMD installed under BN SDP45 6599 for testing in 1984 (see Chapter 6).

But the SD60MAC's real claim to fame is its drive system. Most North American locomotives are equipped with DC drive systems (also known as "DC traction"), which consist of a main generator (or an alternator and rectifiers) supplying variable DC voltage to DC series traction motors. The motors, in turn, use gears to turn the wheels and produce the tractive force needed to haul the train.

But BN's SD60MACs are different. They use an alternator to turn out alternating current (AC), which a three-phase rectifier then converts to direct current (DC). Inverters then "chop" the DC back to AC, which feeds the AC traction motors.

BN struggled to get better reliability with GP50s such as 3136 at La Grange, Ill., in 1989 (above). GP50 3112 (left) sports a modified paint scheme designed to promote grade-crossing visibility.

PAUL D. SCHNEIDER PHOTOS

An AC traction motor is simple compared to its DC counterparts. It has almost no moving parts compared with a DC motor's brushes and commutators. Thus the AC motor offers improved reliability and costs less to maintain than a DC motor. What's more, AC handles harsh operating conditions such as snow and rain better than DC, which translates into lower maintenance costs and higher

reliability. AC also provides improved adhesion and tractive effort, which is the usable force a locomotive's wheels exert at the rails for pulling a train.

The trade-off between AC and DC drive systems is that the AC drive is simple to build but difficult — and complicated — to control. A DC drive, on the other hand, is more complex but controlling it is easier. It all comes down to a matter of

BN's three demonstrator SD60s were returned to EMD, which later leased them to Santa Fe (left) and Soo Line (below).

PAUL D. SCHNEIDER TOP PHOTO
R. BEE BOTTOM PHOTO

trading the complexity of the control system, which is relatively secure inside the locomotive, for the complexity of the traction motor, which is hanging under the carbody being banged at speed.

Despite its purported advantages many North American railroads have been reluctant to sample, let alone commit to, AC traction. Part of the problem is that AC traction can be three times as expensive as a comparable DC system. Most U.S. railroads are notoriously conservative when it comes to new locomotive technology. AC traction is particularly suspect, insomuch as it is seen as some sort of foofy European technology that isn't applicable to the manly world of U.S. railroads. Although CP Rail in Canada equipped a six-motor high-horsepower locomotive with AC traction

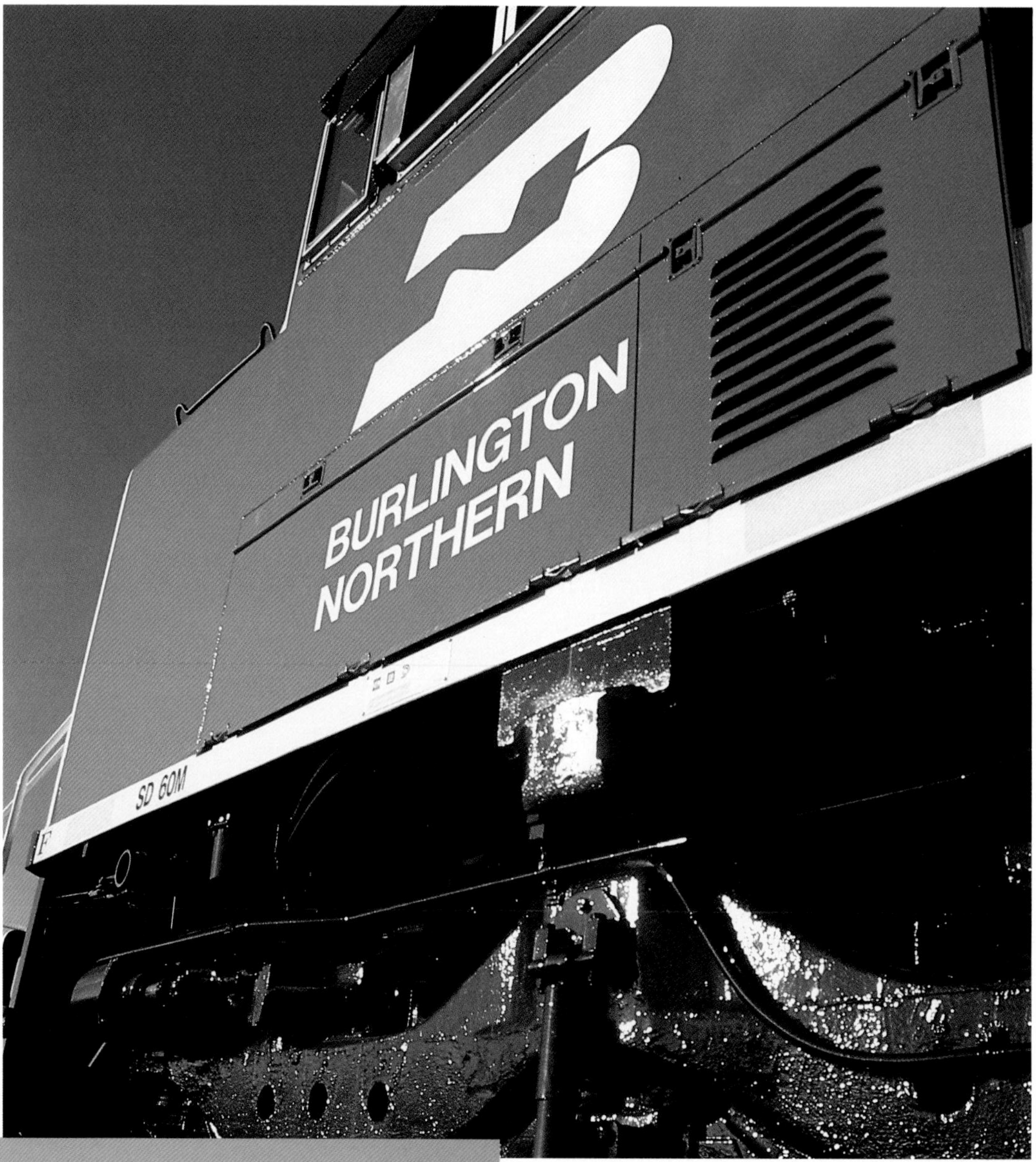

BN's SD60Ms look muscular both at rest (right) and on the point of a unit coal train at Nerco, Mont. (below).

PAUL D. SCHNEIDER TOP PHOTO
KIRK PETTY BOTTOM PHOTO

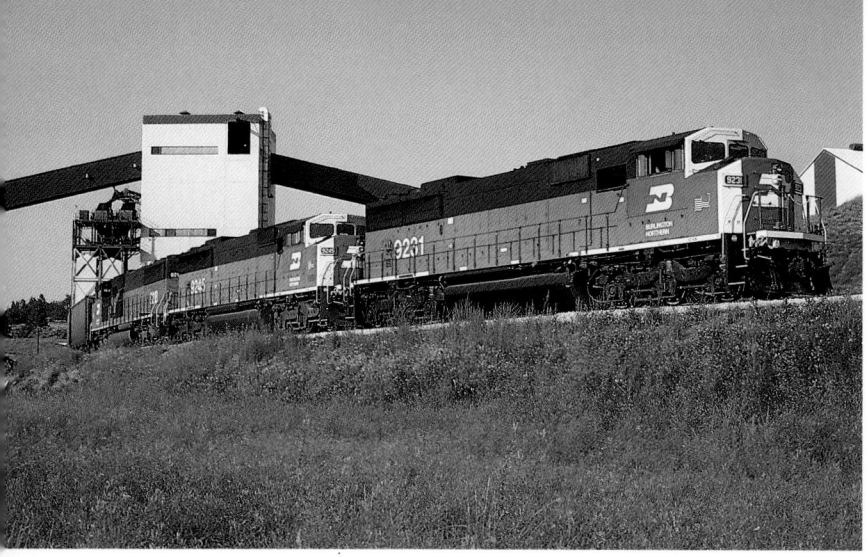

for evaluation, the attitude of most U.S. railroads has been, "Let someone else work out the bugs, then we'll look at it."

BN's four 9500s are proof that the railroad is confident that AC traction is the technology of the future. In 1991 BN General Superintendent-Locomotive Operations Ron Swearengin compared AC traction to the early days of television when a number of "experts" declared that television, while technically feasible, would never be cost-effective. "They recommended against further development, and you can see where television is today," he said. "We're saying that AC traction is the same thing."

Swearengin wasn't kidding. On March 16, 1993, BN announced that it was investing more than $675 million in AC traction locomotives, specifically 350 SD70MACs. The SD70M — which had been introduced by GMLG in 1992 as the successor to the SD60 — packs a 16-cylinder 710G3B diesel engine that cranks out 4,000 h.p. It also sports the same radial trucks as BN's SD60MACs.

Speculation abounds that BN — with its monster order for 350 units — got a price well under that stiff premium usually quoted for AC traction. No matter. BN announced that the first eight SD70MACs would be delivered in 1993, with 60 to 100 additional units to be delivered each year from 1994 until 1997. It only remains to be seen whether BN's SD70MACs will prove to be as technically and economically feasible as television.

ALTHOUGH the SD60MACs and power by the hour units are a giant technological leap forward from the big bombers of the 1970s, both groups of locomotives at least burn (or burned) the

For its second order of SD60Ms, BN chose the paint scheme seen here on 9255 at W. Decker, Mont.
KIRK PETTY PHOTO

The "super cabs" on BN's SD60Ms offer crews a safer, more comfortable work environment.

MIKE ABALOS PHOTO

same fuel: diesel oil.

But not all internal-combustion locomotives run on diesel oil. The first internal-combustion locomotive — built by H. K. Porter, Inc., in 1921 — was fueled by gasoline. Even today, many small industrial-sized switching locomotives — known to many railfans as "critters" — are powered by gasoline engines.

Still, most non-industrial locomotives built after the introduction of EMD's FT diesel in 1939 burn fuel oil. But there are problems with oil, one of the biggest being supply. For example, when an oil-producing nation in the Middle East (Iraq) invades a neighboring oil-producing country (Kuwait), supply suffers, either because Iraq turns off the flow of oil from Kuwait or because Iraq's oil-producing fields are being bombed. Oil has another problem unrelated to whether it is produced by friend or foe: It releases more pollutants than other fuels.

One of those other fuels is natural gas. Not only is natural gas the most abundant fuel around, it burns cleaner. In the early 1990s the U.S. Department of Energy estimated that at current U.S. production rates there was more than a 200-year supply of natural gas. What's more, natural gas prices have long remained stable and are economically more attractive than diesel oil.

BN has long flirted with alternatives to the conventional oil-fueled locomotive. In 1973 it launched a study into the feasibility of electrifying one or more stretches of its mainline trackage in the Powder River basin. General Electric and a handful of other electric locomotive manufacturers were consulted about the possibility of hauling unit trains with straight electric locomotives using overhead catenary for a power distribution system. The study assumed an annual volume of 100

BN 9297 honors 44 BN employees who were called to duty in the 1992 Gulf War.

RIK ANDERSON TOP PHOTO
STEVE GLISCHINSKI BOTTOM PHOTO

million tons of coal shipped in unit trains powered by locomotives of 5,100, 8,400, and 11,000 horsepower. Electric power would be provided by public utilities, many of which, coincidentally, were coal-fired power plants.

What further intrigued BN was the straight electrics' ability to draw almost unlimited power from the overhead wire while accelerating its train. Thus a straight electric could be loaded more heavily than an equivalent diesel and still maintain the same schedule, regardless of stops or speed restrictions. But mainline electrification has one big drawback: cost. Even when BN was toying with the idea in the mid-to-late 1970s, the price to electrify a mile of railroad track was more than $1 million.

A more likely alternative to fuel oil is natural gas. Keeping the Federal Railroad Administration apprised of its work, BN began testing natural gas in 1982. The centerpiece of the project was 1961, a plain-vanilla EMD GP9 retrofitted to burn natural gas by means of a compressed natural gas tube trailer mounted on a flat car coupled to the locomotive. The idea was to develop an alternative that was cheaper and less susceptible to severe price fluctuations than oil.

As it turned out, 1961 had limitations, the most significant being that the horsepower output from natural gas didn't match the output produced by diesel fuel. The test did prove, however, that a locomotive hauling around a tankful of natural gas could be operated safely.

Number 1961's successors are BN SD40-2 7890 and 7149. These six-motor EMDs have been modified to run on either diesel fuel or refrigerated liquid methane, known as RLM, a purer version

EMD's SD70Ms share radial trucks with the four SSD60MACs that BN acquired for testing in 1992.

ELECTRO-MOTIVE DIVISION PHOTO

9500
9500
9501

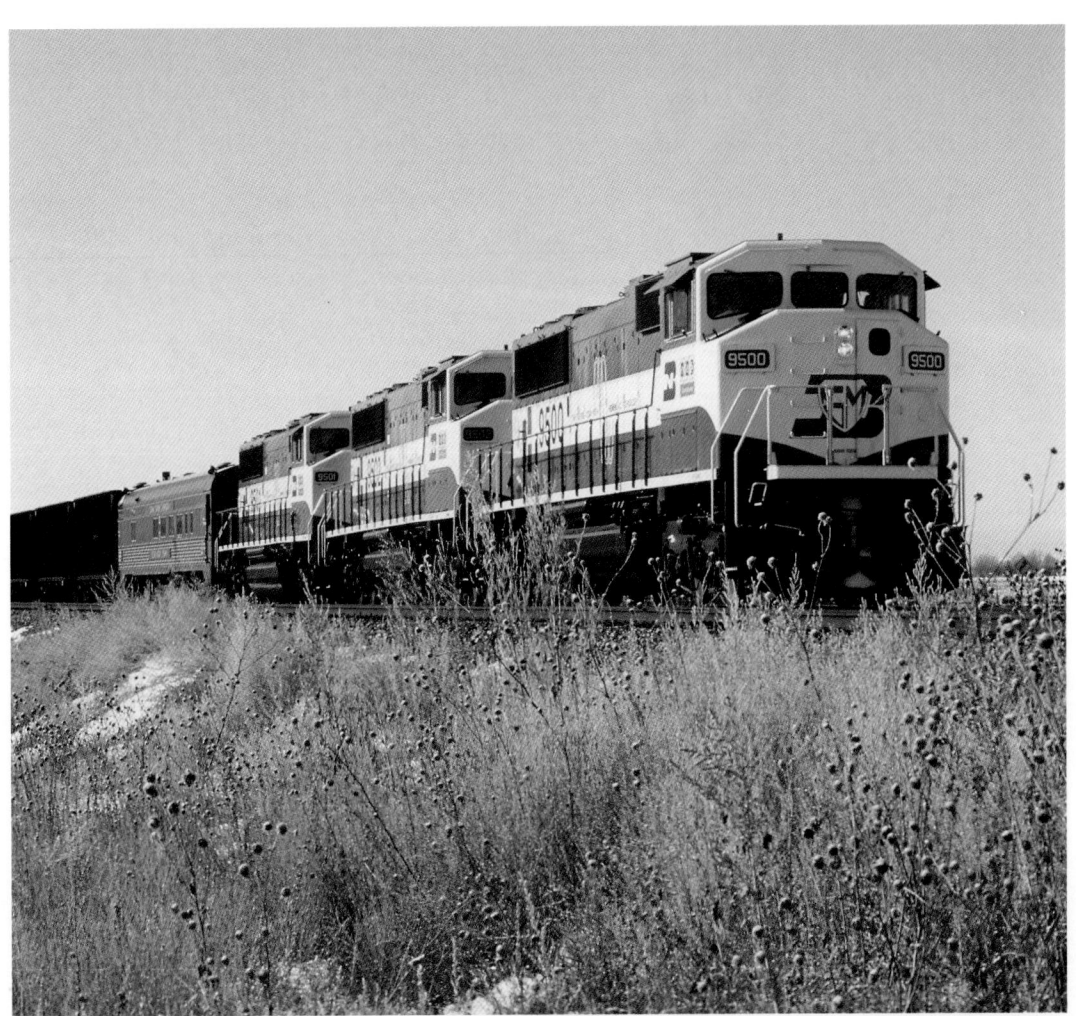

BN's SD60MACs will share an AC drive system with the 350 SD70MACs that BN ordered in 1993.

BURLINGTON NORTHERN PHOTO

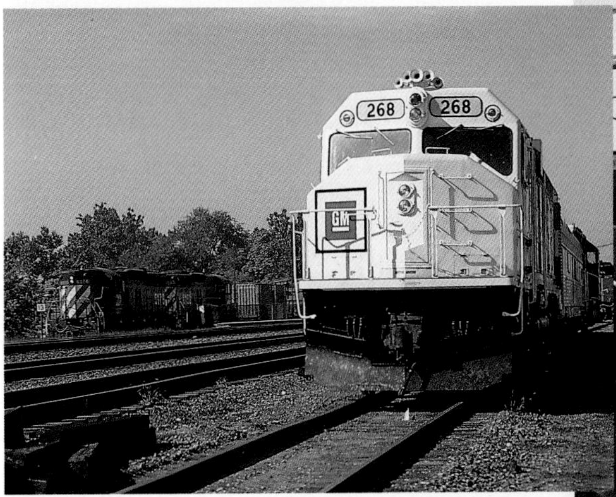
268
268
GM

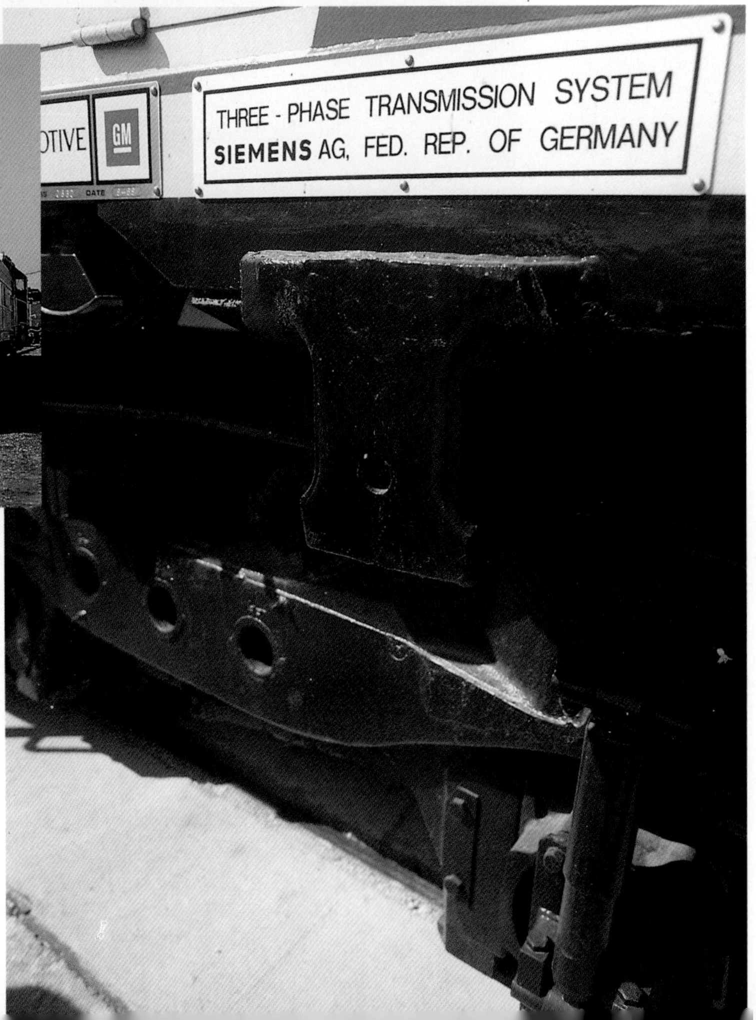
GM
THREE - PHASE TRANSMISSION SYSTEM
SIEMENS AG, FED. REP. OF GERMANY

EMD tested AC traction with No. 268 (above), which is equipped with components from Siemens (right).

PAUL D. SCHNEIDER PHOTOS

BN 1961 may look like a GP9 on the outside (bottom photo) but it burns natural gas drawn from a tube trailer on a flatcar (right).

J.H. LEMKE TOP PHOTO
D.P. HOLBROOK COLLECTION

DAN POITRAS BOTTOM PHOTO

of liquified natural gas.

RLM is a trademark of Air Products & Chemicals of Allentown, Pa., which builds the insulated, pressurized tank cars that keep the gas at temperatures below the minus 260 degrees Fahrenheit required for the fuel to stay liquid. Also involved in the project is Los Alamos-National Laboratory in New Mexico, which has conducted safety studies on the proposal for the locomotive and fuel tender.

Like many fuels, natural gas must be regarded as a hazardous material. However, unlike the liquid propane gas (LPG) used in campers and backyard grills, natural gas is lighter than air and will rise and

Successor to GP9 1961 is SD40-2 7149, which runs on refrigerated liquified methane gas.

SCOTT E. O'DELL PHOTO

disperse when warmed to ambient temperature. The RLM used by BN is so cold that when it is exposed to ambient air it immediately begins to rise. As it rises, it mixes with air and quickly becomes diluted so it is no longer flammable. It also has a narrower flammability range than LPG, which reduces the likelihood of ignition and fire. Since methane has a higher ignition temperature than petroleum products, a fire or explosion is less likely. BN further minimizes the possibility of the gas being released into the atmosphere by using a double-walled tender car with half-inch-thick outer and inner shells.

When BN's natural gas program was reviewed in 1986 it was essential that existing natural gas engine technology be redeveloped to produce the equivalent horsepower of diesel. A dual-fuel engine that could run on either diesel or natural gas and match the diesel version's horsepower was designed, thereby allowing the unit to start on diesel and convert to natural gas automatically.

In 1989 a test engine capable of developing 3,000 h.p. was built. More than 500 hours of testing followed as the engine was cycled through various throttle settings and operated for long periods at full

horsepower to simulate conditions such as stress and high temperatures. Finally in December 1991 7890 and an RLM tender made their debut; they began testing in coal train service between Montana and North Dakota by April 1992. Number

7149 joined 7890 in August 1992, and the two locomotives began operating between Alliance, Neb., and Superior, Wis.

Overall cost savings will be a major factor in BN's decision whether to shift to natural gas. Another factor is that the RLM-fueled locomotives offer improved engine cycle life, which simply means that the RLM engine lasts longer than a comparable diesel engine. Also, fewer fueling stops would be required for natural gas locomotives than for diesel-powered units. The single tender that splices the 7890 and 7149 allows the set to operate at least 1,800 miles without stopping to refuel. Refueling a locomotive costs money, both in terms of the labor involved in yanking the units off of the train, topping off their fuel tanks, and hooking them back up to the train, and the time lost when the locomotive is sitting in the servicing facility instead of out on the road hauling freight.

BN's goal is to have RLM-fueled locomotives power unit coal trains in the Powder River Basin area of Wyoming and Montana, where natural gas prices are among the lowest in the nation. Even with price fluctuations, natural gas is about 20 percent cheaper than diesel fuel.

If BN raises the curtain on RLM-fueled units, you won't see GP9 1961 — or any other low-to-medium-horsepower unit, for that matter — on the stage. Granted, RLM-fueled units burn cleaner and with almost no pollution compared to other fuels, a trait that would seem to make them ideal for locomotives assigned to switching service in urban areas. But BN feels that the greatest economic benefits are realized on locomotives that gulp more fuel than the smaller locomotives used in switching and branchline service. The more fuel a locomotive burns, the more money the railroad saves. By that measure, RLM makes more sense in high-productivity, high-utilization locomotives . . . exactly what BN uses to haul the glut of unit coal trains it operates in the profitable Powder River region.

BN envisions a 4,000 to 6,000 h.p. RLM-fueled locomotive that offers "optimum unit replacement opportunities." Loosely translated from corporate-speak, this means that BN can use three or even two high-horsepower RLM units to lug, say, a 14,000-ton loaded unit coal train that typically rates four 3,000 h.p. C30-7s or SD40-2s or three 3,800 h.p. SD60Ms. Multiply the cost savings realized on that one train by the hundreds of trains that BN operates in the Powder River region, add in the savings in refueling costs, and factor in lower engine wear and its associated maintenace costs, and you'll begin to understand why RLM-fueled locomotives — like power-by-the hour and AC traction — are a key part of BN's ongoing program to push the envelope of big bomber technology.

The shiny plate on the side of BN 7149 tells the story of its conversion to RLM fuel.
PAUL D. SCHNEIDER PHOTO

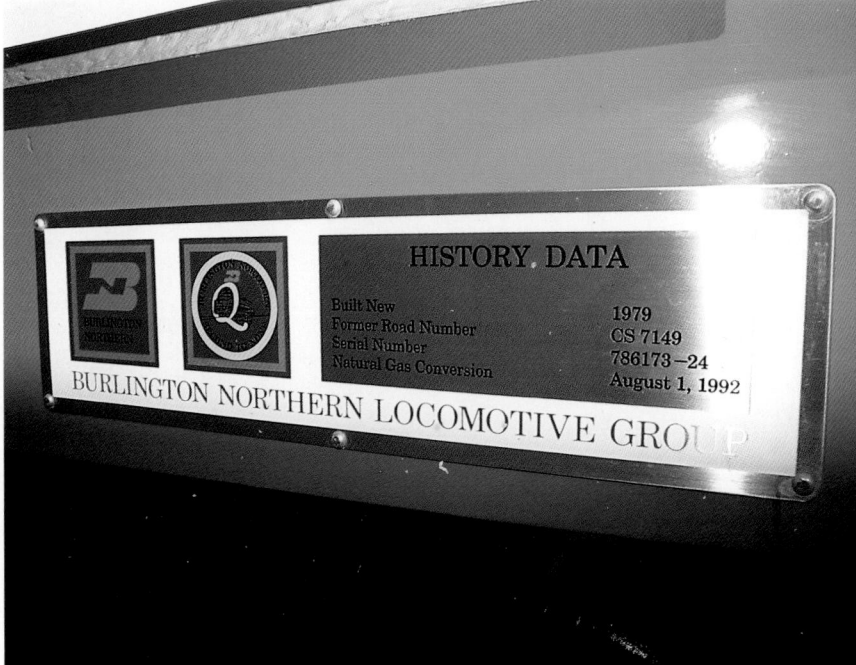

CHAPTER 5

*Solving
medium-horsepower
locomotive problems*

REBUILT AND REBORN

ASK ME WHAT I remember about the locomotives that BN used to assign to its secondary and local trains in the 1970s and I'll tell you in two words: alarm bells.

When a running diesel locomotive experiences a problem, an alarm bell sounds, notifying the crew in the cab that a component has failed, for example, or the unit is running hot. And when I think of locomotive alarm bells, I can't help but think of the Cle Elum Turn.

In the 1970s the Cle Elum Turn was a local train that originated at BN's Auburn (Wash.) terminal and crossed the Cascade Mountains via Stampede Pass to reach the town of Cle Elum. Back then the Cle Elum Turn's power generally consisted of 20- to 30-year-old EMD F units, often operated in multiples of six or seven units because of the 2.2 eastbound grade across Stampede Pass.

Under the distinctive cowling above the cab of GP30 2830 lurks the heart of a rebuilt locomotive.

EMD GP38-2s such as BN 2300 (right) and 2106 at Maupin, Ore., (below) are typical of mid-range, medium horsepower locomotives.

A friend of mine spent several weeks working the first trick operator's job at Auburn in the summer of 1977. He was hunched over the typewriter bashing out train orders one morning when he noticed what sounded like a telephone ringing constantly in the background. "Jesus," he snapped to a signal maintainer who was standing nearby, "why doesn't someone answer that goddam telephone?" To which the signal maintainer said laconically, "That's no telephone. Those are the alarm bells ringing on the Cle Elum Turn's power."

BN WASN'T opposed to buying new locomotives for local and secondary service. The first locomotives delivered in BN paint were six EMD 2,000 h.p. GP38s (actually ordered by SP&S). Then BN sampled 32 copies of the follow-up model, the GP38-2. Once it got a handle on its motive power needs in the Powder River Basin in 1980, BN again signed up for medium-horsepower EMD four-motor

BN's CLRP program in the 1970s turned old GP7s into like-new units such as 1426 at Portland, Ore.

PAUL D. SCHNEIDER PHOTO

units, specifically 40 2,300 horsepower GP39-2s. These were 12-cylinder turbocharged diesels that promised better fuel economy and lower emissions than the 2,000 h.p. 16-cylinder GP38-2.

Despite the popularity of these medi-um-horsepower units on BN, sales were plagued by two factors. For EMD, the profit margin on a GP38-2 or GP39-2 was smaller because each sold for less than its 3,000 horsepower four-motor counterpart, the GP40-2. But as the price of new diesels

climbed in the 1980s BN began to shy away from ordering new medium- horsepower units to power low-priority (and often low-profit) trains.

BN's first alternative to buying new replacement locomotives for low-priority service came in 1974 when it budgeted $5.4 million for its Comprehensive Locomotive Rebuild Program (known as CLRP) at the West Burlington, Iowa, shop. Twenty-three EMD GP7s were rebuilt with upgraded mechanical and electrical components and emerged with chopped-down short hoods (known as "chopped noses"). The rebuilt units were rated at 1,800 h.p. (300 more than their original GP7 rating)

In the 1980s high-horsepower units such as GP40s (above) and GP35s (right) were demoted to secondary service. "Competitive Remanufacturing" transformed GP30 2232 in 1972 into GP39M 2826 in 1990 (opposite page).

F. HOL WAGNER, JR. TOP PHOTO
PAUL D. SCHNEIDER OTHER PHOTOS

A GP35 leads a hot manifest train north on the Oregon Trunk mainline at Maupin, Ore., in 1976.

PAUL D. SCHNEIDER PHOTO

which slotted them into the 1,400 series.

Although the original proposal called for 20 NW2 switchers to be rebuilt, only four were completed. They were all former Great Northern units that emerged as 1,200 h.p. units with similar electrical and mechanical improvements and some external changes. The program proved to be too expensive, however, and BN decided to concentrate its financial resources on — surprise, surprise! — new units for Powder River Basin coal service.

In the early 1980s a short-term answer was provided by BN's new GE B30-7As and EMD GP50s, which bumped older second-generation diesels — mainly EMD GP20s, GP30s, GP35s, and GP40s — from out of the high-horsepower pool and into local and secondary service. By the late 1980s, however, those units were nearing the end of their normal 20- to 30-year life cycle. Worse, they'd all seen better days in terms of fuel economy, repair costs, and reliability.

BN's solution was to enter into what it called "competitive remanufacturing." The program was launched in 1988 and consists of 250 units to be remanufactured over five years. Four-fifths of the units in the program consist of 20- to 30-year-old EMD GP30s, 35s, and 40s upgraded with such updated technology as EMD's Dash 2 electrics and 645 power assemblies. Most of the early rebuilds were drawn from BN's own roster, but as time passed units once owned by railroads as diverse as the Gulf, Mobile & Ohio and Southern Pacific were cranked through the program.

The 2,250 horsepower GP30s and 2,500 horsepower GP35s emerged as 2,300 horse-power units, which BN dubbed "GP39s" in deference to EMD's stock 2,300 h.p. GP39 and GP39-2s. But the stock GP39 and GP39-2 were built with a 12-cylinder 645 engine, while BN's "GP39s" retained their original 16-cylinder 567 engine block.

Initially the candidates for the GP39 portion of the remanufacturing program came from BN's own ranks of GP30s and GP35s, including 33 ex-Frisco GP35s.

Not that you can tell anything about the former identity of BN's GP39s. In 1986 several friends and I practically had a group heart attack when we noticed that the westbound freight we were pacing along US 2 near Skykomish, Wash., contained a former Frisco GP35 equipped with

a pair of Alco AAR Type B trucks and roof-mounted air reservoir tanks. The Type B trucks came from one of the Alco FAs that Frisco had traded in on its GP35s in 1964; the roof-mounted air tanks were the result of a larger-than-normal fuel tank, which pushed the tanks from their usual location above the fuel tank to the roof. Even though the unit we saw was dressed in BN green, not Frisco red and white, we

In the 1980s BN's GP35s were relegated to transfers in Seattle (above) and way-freights in Bellingham, Wash. (below)

PAUL D. SCHNEIDER PHOTOS

EMD built GP50 3158 in 1986, but 2917 (right) made its debut twice: as a GP35 in 1964, then as a GP39E in 1990. M-K rebuilt GP40M 3519 and GP39M 2830 (below). Remanufactured units such as 2830 (opposite page) come with a 3-year warranty and a 20-year life expectancy.

MIKE ABALOS TOP PHOTO
MIKE DANNEMAN OTHER PHOTOS

knew it was a former Frisco unit because none of BN's former Great Northern or Burlington GP35s was equipped with Type B trucks and roof-mounted air tanks.

Today that ex-Frisco unit is indistinguishable from the other GP35s that were recycled through the competitive remanufacturing program. That's because BN specs called for all of the GP39s to be equipped with Blomberg trucks and dynamic brakes. So the Type B trucks under the Frisco units were swapped for the same Blomberg trucks as the other GP35s in the program. The air reservoirs were relocated below the frame. Even a former Louisville & Nashville ACL unit that entered the program without dynamic brakes emerged with dynamic brakes.

The 28 GP40s that emerged from the

program are a much simpler matter. The GP40 rolled out of EMD's plant in McCook, Ill., with a 3,000 h.p. 645-type engine. Because the remanufacturing program called for all units to be equipped with 645 power assemblies, the remanufactured GP40s retain their original engine blocks. The reborn GP40s even keep their original 3,000 h.p. rating. And because the remanufactured GP40s are all ex-BN units inherited from the Burlington, they stepped into the program with dynamic brakes and Blomberg trucks.

REGARDLESS OF the heritage of the units in the program or who performed the work, all of the remanufactured GP39s and GP40s come with a 20-year life expectancy and a three-year warranty that at the time the program was started was better than the two-year new locomotive warranty offered by EMD and GE. Although BN's West Burlington, Iowa, shop was experienced in complete locomotive rebuilds, "competitive" in the new concept meant that the order was open to outside suppliers. The first 50 units were

"Power by the Hour" units such as LMX 8538 and EMD-rebuilt 2929 are innovative solutions to motive power problems.

PAUL D. SCHNEIDER PHOTO

split evenly between Morrison-Knudsen and EMD, but VMV Enterprises of Paducah, Ky., soon entered the fray. You can tell who rebuilt which unit by the suffix BN uses to identify each unit. Thus a GP30E is a GP30 rebuilt by EMD, a GP35V is a GP35 rebuilt by VMV, and a GP40M is a GP40 rebuilt by MK.

There have been ups and downs in the program, including problems with the reliability of some components. But the biggest hurdle the railroad faced came after the competitive remanufacturing program was announced. Seemingly overnight there was a significant jump in the price of components and what BN calls "hulks" (which are GP30s, 35s, and 40s worn out or inoperable). Higher prices for components and hulks threatened to undercut the economic justification of the program, which was BN's polite way of saying that rising prices could have prompted the railroad to discontinue the program. The issue settled down when VMV entered the program armed

with a handy supply of GP30s and GP35s purchased from CSXT and Illinois Central Gulf. The latter, incidentally, were old Gulf, Mobile & Ohio units that were also equipped with AAR Type B trucks from Alco FA trade-ins.

To wrap up the competitive remanufacturing program BN turned its eye to the problem of a low-horsepower four-axle

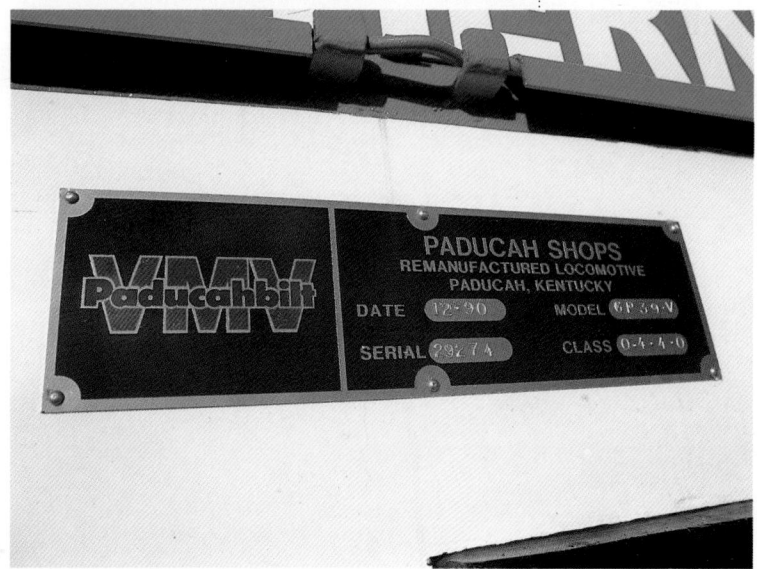

locomotive for branchline and local work. The first inkling of what BN had in mind came in 1991 when BN shipped three GP9s to EMD at McCook, Ill., so that the builder could design a prototype 2,000 h.p. locomotive, which EMD called a "BL20." The "BL" stands for "branchline," one of several uses BN and EMD envisioned for the unit; "20" stood for 2,000 h.p. EMD and BN worked together to develop the specifications for the unit, which made its debut at BN's Railroad Days in Galesburg, Ill., in the summer of 1992. But the testing that was supposed to take place on BN

never happened. EMD people grumbled that BN had promised the moon but came up cash poor when it came time to commit to the units. BN, on the other hand, claimed simply not to be interested in the BL20, although in January 1993 two of the BL20s were leased to BN for use out of the Twin Cities.

Ironically the solution to BN's problem of a low-horsepower branchline locomotive was a GP9 remanufactured by Morrison-Knudsen, one of EMD's competitors, and tagged with the name of one of EMD's own locomotive models, the GP28. The

Four EMD GP9s wait to power a train out of Sumas, Wash., on a snowy December night in 1976.

PAUL D. SCHNEIDER PHOTO

Ex-BN GP9s found homes on Kiamich in Oklahoma (left) and copper Basin in Arizona (below).
ROBERT GALLEGOS PHOTOS

original EMD GP28 made the scene in 1964 with a 567 diesel engine that turned out 1,800 h.p. MK's version takes the GP9's original 567C engine block, upgrades it with 645 components, updates the Geep's old electrical system with Dash 2 components, and stuffs the works into a re-designed carbody that looks a lot like a late-model EMD road-switcher. The resulting units turn out 1,850 h.p., 100 more than the GP9's original rating. BN calls it "a good low-horsepower remanufactured loco," which is probably about as excited as you can get about a recycled locomotive in this horsepower range.

IF ANY LOCOMOTIVE in the medium-horsepower range is worth getting excited about it's probably BN's Caterpillar diesel-powered GP20C. Ten GP20s were transformed by Generation II Locomotive, a company established by Caterpillar dealer Ziegler Inc., of Babbitt, Minn.

The GP20s that were shanghaied for the GP20C project were variously low-nose units inherited from the Burlington and high-nose units from Great Northern. But it's unlikely you'll recognize much of the original diesels in their current state. That's because Gen II doesn't use much of the original unit except for the Blomberg trucks (which are reconditioned) and the main frame. Gen II begins by installing a 16-cylinder Caterpillar 3516 diesel rated at 2,075 h.p. This is one of Cat's 3500 family of engines introduced in 1982.

Next Gen II installs a 1,250-volt brushless/transitionless traction alternator and other electrical equipment supplied by Kato, a unit of Mankato, Minn.-based Reliance Electric. A microprocessor control system that governs engine excitation, wheel slip, and other related functions comes next, followed by the installation of a new inertial and traction motor air system.

The last item is a new cooling system

GP9 1846 went from switching near the U.S.-Canada border at Sumas, Wash., to shortline Pend Oreille Valley.

98

The angular lines of GP9 1922's long hood (left) and the Geep's rounded cab roof (below) will soon vanish from BN.

PAUL D. SCHNEIDER PHOTOS

designed for treated water or antifreeze. This allows the GP20C to be shut down in cold weather, thereby saving fuel. Gen II claims that the GP20C has a 17 to 30 percent fuel advantage over EMD's GP38-2. Simplifying cold-weather shutdowns and start ups is the GP20C's start/stop simplicity, which allows a BN crew member to shut down a GP20C as easily as pressing a button.

Another of the GP20C's assets is its ability to satisfy stricter emission standards. Gen II and BN believe that Gen II's Cat engine has the capacity to meet the tougher controls that are likely to emerge

in the 1990s. Even BN rival Soo Line — a railroad not known for flirting shamelessly with locomotive innovations — has acquired 10 Gen II units, mainly because of concerns about the pollutants generated by diesel locomotives while working in urban areas such as Minneapolis and St. Paul.

BN calls the GP20Cs "versatile" and uses them in everything from intermodal trains to locals. Essentially they are test units, but when asked about the GP20Cs in early 1993, BN Superintendent of Locomotive Operations Dale H. Propp indicated that BN would probably extend the its lease with Gen II. "They've had a lot of modifications," said Propp. "And they [Gen II] have spent some time modifying them."

The GP20Cs aren't BN's first experience with a Caterpillar-powered diesel. In 1986 BN repowered EMD SD40-2 6330 with a 12-cylinder 3,800 h.p. Cat 3612 engine. Grand Trunk Western and a myriad of industrial railroads have successfully repowered old Alco switchers with small 975 h.p. Cat diesels, but attempts to use Cat's 3,800 h.p. 3612 diesel to repower high-horsepower six-motor EMD roadswitchers on BN, C&NW and Santa Fe have generally been less than satisfactory.

The problem, however, may have less to do with the suitability of the Cat engine for railroad applications than with the *way* the railroads have applied it. Repowering a locomotive is like transplanting a human organ: If you want the transplant to take, you have to closely match the blood types of the donor and the organ recipient. That seems to be the reason behind the problems BN has had with 6330, which basically retains most of its original EMD electrical and mechanical components. BN says that if it had the chance to repower the 6330 knowing what

BN's GP9s will remain in local and switching service, but they won't look like this old Geep at La Grange, Ill., in 1989.

PAUL D. SCHNEIDER PHOTO

101

BN's Caterpillar-engined GP20C 2002 leads Soo's Cat-engined 4101 through Daytons Bluff, Minn., in 1993.

it knows today, it would follow Gen II's lead and design a system to support the Cat engine. For Gen II and Caterpillar, the larger question is: When BN decides to order new medium-horsepower units in the future will it order more Caterpillar-engined diesels knowing what it knows about the Gen IIC today?

Two solutions to the problem of mid-range diesels: Gen II's 2,000 h.p. GP20C (left) and MK's 1,800 h.p. GP28 (below).

JERRY GUNDERSON TOP PHOTO
STEVE GLISCHINSKI BOTTOM PHOTO

CHAPTER 6

*Locomotive-related
experiments*

SLUGS AND OTHER ODDITIES

FOR THE FIRST 12 YEARS after the 1970 merger the most unusual BN locomotives weren't locomotives at all. They were slugs, specifically ET-1, ET-2, and ET-3. The idea behind the locomotive slug is explained in Chapter 3, so I needn't repeat it here. Suffice to say that ET-1, ET-2, and ET-3 were yard slugs BN called "electric trailers." Northern Pacific built them from the hulks of three retired Baldwin switchers between 1959 and 1965 for use on its hump yard at Pasco, Wash.

Between 1987 and 1988 the three slugs were retired without fanfare. ET-1 and ET-2

Look ma, no cab! General Electric B30-7A rolls through Chicago, Ill., in April 1991.
PAUL D. SCHNEIDER PHOTO

BN's ET slugs swapped their NP colors in Pasco, Wash., in 1972 (right) for BN green in Duluth, Minn., in 1985 (below).

PAUL D. SCHNEIDER TOP PHOTO
OTTO P. DOBNICK BOTTOM PHOTO

went directly to scrap. ET-3, on the other hand, landed a home on iron-ore hauler Duluth, Missabe & Iron Range, which renumbered it 500, repainted it into DM&IR colors, and soon stored it when it didn't meet the railroad's expectations. It wasn't until several years after the passing of ET-1, ET-2, and ET-3 that I once again heard talk about BN slugs — except that this time it was about BN's cabless GE B30-7As.

In truth, the B30-7As can't, by any wild stretch of the imagination, be considered true slugs. But that didn't matter to my friend, Steve Hart. The B30-7As lacked cabs, so as far as he was concerned, they were less than a real locomotive. To Hart's way of thinking, the cabless GEs had more in common with ET-1, ET-2, and ET-3.

Of course, there's nothing all *that* unusual about cabless diesels. After all, the first successful road diesel — Electro Motive's FT 103 — was composed of two FT cab units (known as "A units") spliced by two cabless FT boosters (or "B unit"). EMD went on to build several thousand F unit cabless boosters, as did EMD's competitors. In the 1950s Union Pacific and a handful of other railroads took the cabless concept a step further by ordering new EMD GP-style road-switchers without cabs. UP was thought to have brought the concept to an end when it ordered its dou-

ble-engined, eight-axle DD35Bs from EMD in the mid-1960s.

Why eliminate the cab on a diesel locomotive? Cost. Climb aboard a locomotive cab and you'll find the controls that the engineer uses to operate the locomotive (or several units coupled into a multiple-unit consist). You'll also find the seats where the crew sits, a water cooler, a cab heater (and, on railroads such as Santa Fe, a cab air-conditioner), and a toilet. Naturally, these items crank up the cost of a new locomotive. And maintaining the cab — sweeping it out, dumping the toilet, stocking it with supplies for the crew — costs money too.

BN certainly was no stranger to cab-

ET-3 changed colors one more time when it became Duluth, Missabe & Iron Range No. 500.
ROBERT C. ANDERSON PHOTO

less units. At the time of the 1970 merger it inherited a fleet of F3Bs, F7Bs, and F9Bs from Great Northern and Northern Pacific. But the railroad got caught up in a cabless craze in the early 1980s. It began with BN's decision in 1980 to rebuild wrecked GE U30C 5336 into cabless U30C 800 (later renumbered to 4500). A year later the railroad rebuilt wrecked EMD SD40 6303 into cabless 7600. BN then rebuilt three wrecked SD40-2s into cabless units and slotted them into the 7500-series number group.

Nor were four-axle units immune. GP38AC 2600 was converted to EMD Dash 2 specs and rebuilt with its cab intact but its numberboards and windows covered up, a sure fire way to discourage the folks in the operating department from tacking the unit on to the point of a train. It eventually regained its cab and was renumbered 2136. Number 2601, on the other hand, was rebuilt without a cab and stayed that way.

Four GP9s were also rebuilt as cabless units and slotted into the 600 series. They worked in hump service spliced by SD7s, where they replaced another group of four-axle booster units, F9Bs. One GP9B, 604, was later fitted with radio remote control and equipped with an operator's shelter, which seems to serve the same function as a (ahem) locomotive cab. Another cabless unit assigned to switch service is 442, which began life as a normal SW1000 before it was wrecked and rebuilt as a cabless SW1000.

Of course, BN isn't alone when it comes to rebuilding wrecked locomotives without cabs. Santa Fe, for example, has rebuilt several SD45s and SD45-2s without cabs. Even the case of the 2600 isn't unique. Missouri-Kansas-Texas, for example, converted F7A cab unit 66C to booster unit 401B by simply plating over its cab windows and number-boards. What *was* unexpected was BN's decision in 1982 to place

Cabless GP9s such as 602 replaced cabless Fs on the Northtown hump yard in Minnesota.
OTTO P. DOBNICK PHOTO

At least the lead unit on train 100 at Marshall, Wash., (left) has a cab. Lack of a cab on 7502 leaves a lot of room for BN's logo.

BRUCE KELLY TOP PHOTO
PAUL D. SCHNEIDER BOTTOM PHOTO

an order for a cabless version of a locomotive: GE's B30-7A.

BN already owned eight B30-7s inherited in 1980 from the Frisco. But those units employed 16 cylinders to turn out their 3,000 h.p., while the B30-7As that BN ordered turned out the same horsepower using 12 cylinders. Using four fewer cylinders means greater fuel efficiency (the same way that a four-cylinder gasoline automobile engine uses less fuel than a six-cylinder engine) and lower maintenance costs (because there are fewer cylinders to maintain).

But BN's cabless B30-7As saved even more money. Right off the bat, BN saved $50,000 over the cost of comparable cab-equipped B30-7A. The cost-saving advantage of the cabless unit was also the reason behind Santa Fe's decision in 1991 to order 23 cableless GP60Bs from builder General Motors Locomotive Group. The B units allow Santa Fe to create a cab/booster/cab locomotive set, much like the FT 103 demonstrator set.

Cost savings aside, BN is unlikely to go the cableless route again. The railroad feels that it loses flexibility with cableless units in terms of crew accommodations and turning consists . . . the same concerns, ironically, that spelled the demise of the cableless diesel locomotive in the first place.

THE HISTORY of BN's locomotives contains two other locomotive-related oddities, neither of which my friend Hart ever nicknamed: the HTBB "self-steering" truck and the fuel tender.

The radial trucks under BN's SD60MACs weren't the first self-steering locomotive trucks to make an appearance on BN. In 1984 EMD developed a self-steering articulated truck it dubbed HTBB (for "High Traction B-B"). Normally a B-B truck des-

ignation means that a locomotive has four axles divided between two trucks. But the HTBB was actually a single truck boasting four axles. Unlike the rigid four-axle Flexicoil truck found under EMD's DD35/DDA35 and DDA40X models (which caused excessive wheel flange and rail wear problems), the HTBB truck employed a two-piece side frame that rotated around a central pedestal.

BN's interest in the project took the shape of SDP45 6599, which traded the conventional three-axle Flexicoil truck at the rear of its carbody for the HTBB

The yoke on BNFT 44 (right) is a flange lubricator; BNFT 23 (below) was under construction at Superior, Wis., in 1984.

D.P. HOLBROOK TOP PHOTO
PAUL A. BERGEN PHOTO

truck. To fit the new truck the SDP's original 5,000-gallon fuel tank was swapped for a 4000-gallon tank. To circumvent substantial modifications to the 6599's electrical system, the middle traction motor on the lead Flexicoil truck was disconnected, technically making the 6599 an A1A (the 1 stands for "idler")-BB unit. As if to call attention to the experiment 6599 emerged from its modification with silver trucks.

With BN SD38-2 6261 and EMD SD45X 5740 along to serve as drag units, 6599 headed to Auburn, Wash., in August 1984 to begin tests on BN over the Cle Elum Turn's old haunt, Stampede Pass (which had been closed to traffic the year before). Testing took place for several weeks in September, after which the unit was supposed to return to EMD to be changed back to its original C-C truck configuration. But for reasons known only to BN and EMD — and even then, who knows? — 6599 stayed in system-wide general freight service until March 1987. Then the HTBB truck was swapped out for a conventional three-axle truck with nary a squeak of comment from EMD or BN. As for 6599 it didn't linger long in the spotlight after being shorn of its B-B-B-B truck; a few weeks later, after it was restored to its rightful six-axle appearance, the 6599 joined BN's other 20-cylinder EMDs in retirement.

LET'S GET one thing straight about BN's fuel tenders: The idea for the program was not inspired by the Elvis Presley song "Love Me Tender."

The function of a fuel tender is to supply fuel to a locomotive at each end of the

BN's fuel tenders in the Powder River Basin may be joined someday by natural gas tenders.

MIKE DANNEMAN PHOTO

The concept of the diesel fuel tender was first advanced by Amtrak 400, seen here in Seattle in 1978.

PAUL D. SCHNEIDER PHOTO

tender. One of the advantages of a fuel tender is that you can fill it with fuel oil at point A and operate a train without having to tank up the locomotives at point B with more expensive fuel. Another benefit is that locomotives stationed at remote locations can remain in the field for longer periods of time before they have to head back to a refueling station for a fill-up.

One of the first fuel tenders converted from an existing piece of rolling stock was Amtrak 400. The small fuel tanks on Amtrak's EMD F40s required frequent fuel stops on Amtrak's long-distance trains, which meant longer schedules. To make matters worse, Amtrak made payments to the freight railroads it contracted with for the maintenance of those railroads' fuel facilities and their EPA-mandated track pans and skimming plants. Amtrak's answer to both problems was to strip the mechanical and electrical guts out of E8A 400 and stuff the space with six 1,350-gal-

lon fuel tanks. The resulting conversion boosted the fuel capacity of the two F40s to 9,300 gallons, enough for a Chicago to Seattle trip — which is where Amtrak tested the 400.

In the end Amtrak chose not to pursue the fuel tender concept. But four years later BN (over whose tracks Amtrak operates between Minneapolis and Seattle) breathed new life into the fuel tender concept when it converted a former CB&Q tank car to fuel tender BNFT-1. The conversion was cheap — just $13,000 — and simple. Basically the modification consisted of installing a filler adapter to allow refilling of the tank car at locomotive fueling stations, sight glasses to measure fuel levels, tank vents, locomotive fuel hoses with connections and gate valves at each end, and pass-through cables and air pipes for MU (multiple-unit) operation. The latter modification allowed locomotives — initially four ex-passenger service

SDP40s — to be placed on either end of the fuel tender in power consists.

BNFT made its initial tests on intermodal trains operating between Chicago and Seattle. The tests showed that five fuel stops could be eliminated and running times improved. But what brought the widest smile to BN's face was a fuel-cost saving of $3,000 per trip. Love me tender indeed.

Eventually 78 fuel tenders were constructed, all from company tank cars. Most were converted from a variety of company tank cars by BN's shops on the Denver Region at Alliance and Havelock, Neb.; and on the Twin Cities Region at Northtown, St. Cloud, Minn., and Superior, Wis. Berwind Railway Services, a contract railroad supplier, converted BNFT 49 through BNFT 78.

One of the most significant variations was found on BNFT 40-46, which were equipped with flange lubrication devices. The idea behind flange lubrication is to produce a slight savings in fuel as well as decreasing flange and wheel wear, especially on curves. Nonetheless, BN subsequently stopped using the flange lubricators on its seven fuel tenders.

Eventually the fuel tenders themselves fell from grace with BN management. Several tenders experienced structural problems due to the tremendous pushing and pulling they were subjected to. And while it is a time-honored tradition for railroaders to gripe about their jobs, train-crews working the head end of trains operating with fuel tenders had more than their share of complaints. The main gripe: The fuel tenders made it difficult to go back to the trailing units in the consist to deal with mechanical and electrical problems unless the train was stopped. BN management has since conceded that in general freight service there was some concern by its operating people about switching the tender in and out of power consists.

Ultimately the one thing that lowered the boom on fuel tenders in general freight service between Chicago and Seattle was the main reason they were built in the first place: the price of diesel fuel. In 1981 BN coughed up a staggering $600 million dollars for diesel fuel. But seven years later the tab for fuel was much less traumatic: $288 million.

With those figures in mind BN in 1989 began converting fuel tenders to 973500-series bulk-fuel tank cars. By 1992 BN rostered only 26 or so fuel tenders, all of which were assigned to the Powder River Basin for use with locomotive helper sets. Of course, if BN launches a fleet of RLM-fueled locomotives for train service in the Powder River Basin, fuel tenders will become a fact of life. I can hear the train crews complaining already.

BN relocated the dynamic brake blisters on SD40B 7600, which was later acquired by Soo Line.

DAN POITRAS PHOTO

CHAPTER 7

*Pre-merger
units that
live on*

THE
SURVIVORS

OVER THE YEARS BN has spent a lot of time and paint assimilating the locomotives from the Great Northern; Northern Pacific; Chicago, Burlington & Quincy; Spokane, Portland & Seattle; and St. Louis - San Francisco into a cohesive BN locomotive fleet. But paint and a comprehensive renumbering scheme didn't fool the white-haired BN engineer I met in Superior, Wis., in 1982. He told me how one day he was called for a westbound train out of Superior with 145 cars, all empties. Worse yet, the power for the train consisted of one unit. When I asked him what happened he shrugged his shoulders and said that he just pulled the throttle back as far as it would go and left it there in the eighth notch for the entire trip. Didn't the unit stall, I asked? "Oh no," he said, "Those sonsabitches were geared real low for that. It was one of those morphodite Great

Seven months after the 1970 merger, a worker in Denver applies a fresh coat of BN paint to a switcher.

F. HOL WAGNER, JR. PHOTO

116

An NP engineer
in Superior didn't
need GN paint
(right) or GN Class
SD7 plates (below)
to identify ex-GN
SD7s and 9s.

WILLIAM BEDELL TOP PHOTO
COLLECTION OF OTTO P. DOBNICK
ROBERT GALLEGOS BOTTOM PHOTO

Northern engines with the three-driver truck." How did he know that a BN green SD7 was a former GN engine? Because he came to the BN from the NP, GN's arch-rival in northern Minnesota. He knew that GN preferred the six-motor SD7s for shoving iron ore on the ore dock in Superior, while NP preferred four-motor Alco RS11s.

For the most part the diesels that the five predecessors brought to the merger were relatively indistinguishable from each other once they were dipped in Cascade green paint and slapped with BN numbers. It was hard, for example, to tell a former GN SD45 from an NP, CB&Q, or Frisco SD45. On the other hand, each predecessor railroad contributed locomotives that were distinctive to that particular railroad.

Those NP RS11s, for example, were unique to NP. NP also contributed BN's

only 251-engine Alco switcher, S6 950. And while SP&S rostered Alco S2 switchers at the time of the merger, only NP owned Alco S4s. NP's two Alco RS1 road-switchers also hung around long enough to receive BN numbers. As for four-motor EMD units, only NP owned 1,800 h.p. GP18s, all delivered with high noses.

GN, Burlington, and SP&S all brought EMD F units to the merger. But only NP

BN carried on GN's practice of using six-motor SD7s and 9s for shoving ore at Superior, Wis.

RONALD A. PLAZZOTTA PHOTO
COLLECTION OF J. DAVID INGLES

had F9 cab units. And NP brought the rarest F units of all: Two EMD FTs, the same model locomotive as EMT FT103, generally considered to be the first successful commercial road freight diesel locomotive. Although they never received their assigned BN numbers (798 for the cab unit, 799 for the booster), both units survived several months past the March 3, 1970, merger. NP also fielded the only

FP7s (the passenger version of the F7A) and the only Baldwins to wear BN numbers, 18 VO1000 switchers, one four-axle DRS4-4-1500, and one six-axle DRS6-6-1500. And if the Baldwins weren't rare enough, four of the VO1000s had been repowered by NP in the late 1950s with EMD engines, making these units the only repowered diesels to work for BN.

As mentioned, SP&S owned several

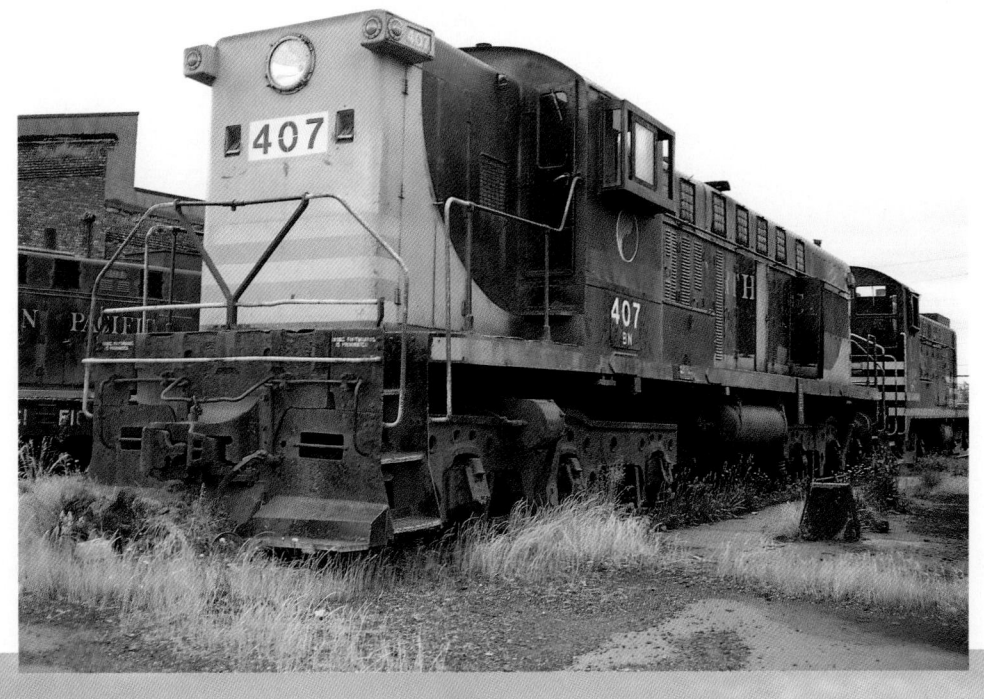

Thanks to NP, BN operated six-motor Baldwins (left) and a pair of Alco RS1s (below).

J. DAVID INGLES PHOTOS

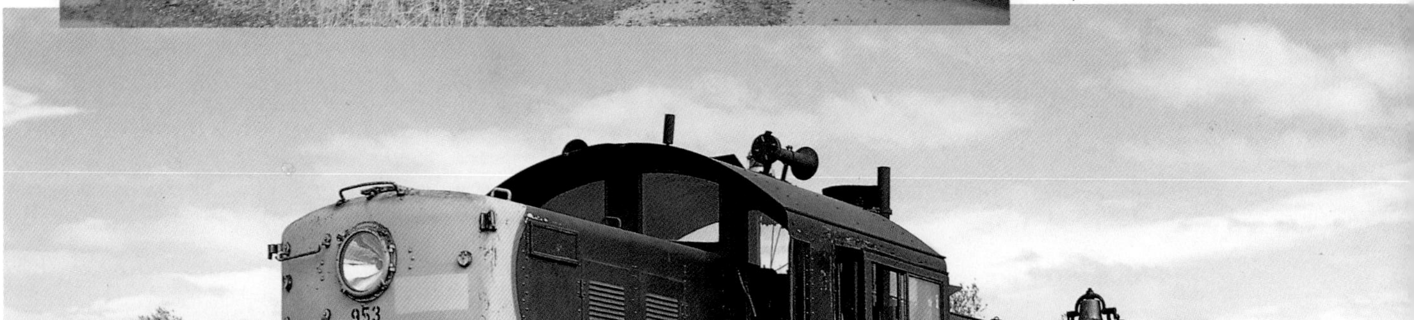

Alco 539-engine switchers at the time of the merger. But only SP&S contributed an S1 — No. 11 — to BN's fleet. And while both SP&S and NP brought RS3s to the roster, BN's only RS2s belonged to SP&S. But the locomotives that any SP&S old head worth his or her salt could recognize regardless of their BN numbers or paint were SP&S' original Century-series locomotives: seven C424s, 16 C425s, 10 C636s, and a pair of funky C415s. Like NP, SP&S also contributed some of the rarest cab units to the BN locomotive fleet: 11 Alco 1,500 h.p. FA1s and one 1,600 h.p. FA2.

Like NP, the Burlington owned an EMD F unit that survived for several months after the merger, although it

The SP&S herald on BN 4246 (top photo,opposite page) is almost redundant; only SP&S brought four-motor Century-series Alcos like 4256 (above) to BN's locomotive fleet.

never officially received its BN number: CB&Q 168A, which was to become BN 796. But Burlington's other cab-unit contributions were just as distinctive as NP's FTs and SP&S' FAs: EMD E8s and E9s, which you can read about in detail in Chapter 8.

EMD's 1,000 h.p. NW2 switcher hailed from all five of the predecessor rail-roads. But only the Burlington had the 1,000 h.p. EMD SW1000. Burlington also contributed the smallest and perhaps most unusual switchers: three GE 44 tonners. Other GEs unique to the Q were BN's nine U23Cs, which the Burlington purchased in 1969 for service on Crawford Hill in Nebraska. Burlington subsidiary Colorado & Southern also rostered four

U30Cs, essentially the 3,000 h.p. version of the 2,300 h.p. U23C.

BN's 3000-series GP40s also trace their heritage to the Q. The 16 EMD SD24s came from Burlington, which also contributed the only low-nose GP20s. And the C&S supplemented its fleet of six-motor high-horsepower units with 13 3,000 h.p. EMD SD40s.

Unlike their sister units from the Burlington, Great Northern's GP20s came with high hoods (and were built to operate long-hood forward). GN shared C&S' taste for the SD40 with one slight difference: GN's units were SDP40s built with steam generators for passenger service, the only such units built for a U.S. railroad. GN must have been pleased with the concept of a high-horsepower six-motor freight

GN, NP and SP&S contributed EMD Fs to BN, but only SP&S kicked in Alco FAs such as FA1 4104.

PAUL D. SCHNEIDER PHOTO

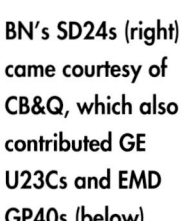

BN's SD24s (right) came courtesy of CB&Q, which also contributed GE U23Cs and EMD GP40s (below).

PAUL D. SCHNEIDER TOP PHOTO
F. HOL WAGNER BOTTOM PHOTO

unit modified for passenger train service because it followed up the SDP40s with eight 3600 h.p. SDP45s.

Perhaps the locomotives most likely to ring the chimes of an old GN engineer were BN's 10 NW5s, all of which traced their heritage to GN. The NW5 was basically an NW2 fitted with road trucks and a steam generator in a short hood behind the cab. GN also brought a handful of old EMD switchers, rebuilt to SW8 and SW900 specs, to BN's locomotive fleet.

When the Frisco merged with BN in 1980 it had long since retired its last FAs, F units, E units and re-engined Alcos and Baldwins. The Frisco units that you can recognize regardless of their paint and numbers are the four SD38-2s, 25 GP15s, and five MP15s. There are two other models that most ex-Frisco engineers and

CB&Q's EMD SW1000s were only five years old when they vanished into BN's diesel fleet.

J. DAVID INGLES PHOTO

roundhouse people recognize as some of their own: B30-7s 5485-5492 (BN's only GE four-motor Dash 7 units) and GP35s 2550-2582. The latter were distinguished from comparable GN and Burlington GP35s by their roof-mounted air reservoirs and, in the case of several units, their Alco AAR Type B road trucks. BN's only GP40-2s and GP38ACs also came from the Frisco, which also sprang for 10 GP50s on the eve of the 1980 merger. GP50 3100 was actually delivered in Frisco paint; it was renumbered into the first slot of the 3100-series that would eventually comprise BN's later GP50s.

Today's BN locomotive fleet is a long way from March 3, 1970, when the first units to wear Cascade green were a handful of former Burlington units and six new

The smallest units CB&Q brought to BN were three GE 44-tonners (below); the sleekest were the Q's silver E8As and E9As (right).

EMD's AC-rectified-equipped GP38AC was unique to Frisco, which contributed 29 units to BN in 1980.

PAUL D. SCHNEIDER PHOTO

EMD GP38s (which had been ordered by SP&S and were delivered at the last minute in BN paint and numbers). BN can now boast of retiring units such as U30Cs and SD40-2s that were ordered by and delivered to BN (older units ordered by one of the predecessor railroads). But as the list that follows shows, there were still a respectable number of pre-merger units (pretty much in their original as-built configuration) hammering around on BN rails as of January 1, 1993.

GN's unique diesels spanned 1000 h.p. NW5s (above) and 3000 h.p. passenger-service SDP40s (left).

DAVE CHORNELL TOP PHOTO
COLLECTION OF F. HOL WAGNER, JR.
J. DAVID INGLES BOTTOM PHOTO

CHAPTER 8

E's and F's in the '80s — and beyond

NEVER SAY DIE

THE BEST STORY I ever heard about BN's F units was the one brakeperson Jerry Johnson told me while we were standing around BN's Belknap Yard in Superior, Wis., with conductor Gene Hill one frigid March night in 1982. The way Johnson told it, he was standing in the yard one night near the scales where BN weighed freight cars, waiting to line what he *thought* was his power on top of his train, when he saw a string of covered wagons — F units, that is — looming at him out of the dark.

"The thing is," Johnson said, "the switch isn't lined for the yard, it's lined for the scales. So I line it the other way, you know, thinking this must be the power for our train. I just took it for granted, those old covered wagons have been around for so long. Well, turned out they were being weighed. For scrap. They were being shipped to a

Who would have believed that the graceful lines of EMD's E's and F's would survive on BN into the 1990s?

Three F-unit paint schemes were on display together in Superior, Wis., in 1974 (above). Five freight F's and a pair of Geeps power the Cle Elum Turn as it crawls up Stampede Pass in 1978 (opposite page).

RAYMOND F. KUCABA PHOTO, ABOVE
BLAIR KOOISTRA PHOTO, FACING PAGE

scrapyard in Duluth. Surprised the hell outta me, I'll tell you."

"Yeah," said Hill, shaking his head. "I remember someone saying once how an A/B/B/A set of covered wagons would be rare someday. And now they are."

Indeed. Some 284 EMD F units showed up at the reception after the GN, NP, Burlington, and SP&S exchanged their 1970 wedding vows. Although the last Burlington F unit (F7A 168A) and the last U.S. FTs (NP 5409D and 5404C) were retired before receiving their official BN numbers (796, 798, and 799 respectively), most of the F's from were rechristened with

BN numbers and, in many cases, a coat of BN Cascade green paint.

During the first few years of the merger the F's were likely candidates for trade-ins on new power. But by the mid-1970s BN was so short of power that F-unit retirements slowed, then stopped. In fact, things were so desperate on the motive power front that BN in 1974 returned to revenue freight service six ex-SP&S F units that had been bumped into maintenance-of-way service in 1972 as power units for electric-powered rotary snowplows. The F's were essentially intact locomotives that had had their traction motors removed and dipped in BN's MoW "mineral red" paint.

Passenger-service F's released from Amtrak service in 1974 were quickly renumbered into the 700 series and slapped into freight service. But the most surprising twist came in 1975 when BN began overhauling F units with the intention of keeping the units in service another five years. For an F-unit in 1975, five years was a lifetime, especially when you consider that other western Class 1 railroads — SP, for example — had long since booted F units from their rosters.

The F-unit fleet stabilized at 116 units for the rest of the decade. Over half of these were assigned to the Seattle and Portland Regions in the Pacific Northwest, where BN felt that the time-worn F's would be taxed less by mild Pacific Northwest winters. The remainder of the fleet, on the other hand, was assigned to the Twin Cities Region in the upper Midwest, where BN felt that the F's were well-suited to the severe winters. The contradiction in assignments proved one thing, at least: The Fs were versatile.

The beginning of the end for the F's came in 1980 when BN slapped a "for sale" sign on 42 units based in the Pacific Northwest and sold most for scrap. On the Twin Cities Region a die-hard group of 24 F's (mostly ex-NP F9s) continued to roam a triangle with vertices at Superior, Wis., Minneapolis, Minn., and Minot, N.D., as late as November 1981. But by the time I showed up in Superior four months later there were just three BN F units in service, all boosters: two units sandwiched between a pair of SD7s in switch service on the hump at Northtown Yard near Minneapolis and 769 in road service out of Superior.

Although the number of F's may have

dwindled on the Twin Cities Region, their presence remained strong in the minds of the BN people at Superior who had worked with them. Take John Cincoski, the affable first-trick roundhouse foreman at Superior. Over a cup of coffee that first morning he told me he'd been more or less raised with the F's after he'd hired out as a laborer at Mississippi Street shops in St. Paul on the Northern Pacific in September 1945.

"I always liked the covered wagons," he told me, "except that when they became older they could be hard to maintain. They were lube oil leakers. And they were bait for the federal men (Federal Railroad Administration). The feds just loved the covered wagons because they knew that if they walked inside of one, they were gonna be walking through a puddle of oil. Another thing about them were the carbodies. There were holes in the floors and in the walls and the snow in the winter would blow in the holes and get into the main generator and *then* you had trouble. Ground relays, which is where the moisture shorts out the wiring inside the main generator. They were great accumulators of snow, the covered wagons! You'd be walking through snowdrifts going alongside of the engine."

Then there were Arvid Brandt and Jim Hansen, a couple of straight-shooting engineers I met while sitting around the big wooden table in the engineer's locker room inside the Superior roundhouse. Brandt and Hansen conceded that the F's were a good engine in their day, but they were just worn out. From there they launched into a litany of complaints about the F's: steps below the cab door that were too narrow for safe footing when getting in and out of the cab; controls that were too far out of the engineer's way (which forced the engineer to twist around to look backwards); and a noisy cab, the result of the F-unit's cab being part of the carbody.

What really irked them, though, was the F's tendency to leak oil and break crankcase shafts, known as throwing a rod.

"Something was always dripping," Brandt snapped, seemingly on the verge of throwing a rod himself. "We brought some back from Duluth a few weeks ago off of 158. I went through the units and all

F's like F9A 776 (opposite page) were little better than a steam engine in the eyes of at least one BN engineer in Superior, Wis. Crews working in the upper Midwest said that the cabs of the old F's (below) were warm in the wintertime.

BLAIR KOOISTRA PHOTO, BELOW

I would've had to do was push from the back and I coulda slid all the way to the front.

"And crankcase explosions. Holy Christ! We went through that continuously! That was a rule, as a fireman, that you had to go back every hour and look at your engines, see if you got any lube oil coming out of your exhaust. Well hey, when you work 16 hours it gets to be a pretty long goddam day."

Hansen nodded. "You get alarm bells and look back and see that she's pre-e-e-etty foggy back there."

"Your airbox covers, they'll blow," said Brandt. "Blows them right the hell off. A lot of guys have come close to getting killed inside them bastards."

"On a hood unit you've got something between you and the explosion," said Hansen. "You're not right inside with it when it happens."

Hansen and Brandt agreed that any of the newer EMD hood units were Cadillacs compared to the covered wagons. Would they miss the F's when they were finally gone? "Not a bit!" roared Brandt. "You can start scrapping them all right now. They were better than a steam engine" — He waved his hand in a throwaway gesture — "but that's about it."

Later that afternoon I hooked up with the crew of train 127, the daily through freight between Superior and Minot, N.D. Cincoski had arranged to lash the 769 into 127's power consist to balance a locomotive shortage in Minot, and I arranged to ride 127 as far west as Cass Lake, Minn., the first crew change west of Superior. Train 127's engineer that afternoon was Fred Levin, another veteran BN engineer who compared the F's to steam engines. In the cab of 127's lead SD40-2 Levin remembered the F's as being "warm in the wintertime. They'd go to beat hell if you got a train that

they could handle. They were like a steam engine almost."

My central memory of that night hinges on a brief trip I made back to the inside of the 769 to get an idea of what the inside of an F unit was like at speed. The roar of the engine hit me like a wet fist the moment I pushed open the door at the rear of the carbody and stepped inside the F. The air was thick with haze and the smell of hot metal. I was thinking about walking through the unit to get a sense of what Brandt and Hansen had been talking about back at Superior when I noticed the lube oil bleeding around the floor near the base of the engine. How fast were we going anyway? The last time I'd checked the speedometer in the cab of the trailing SD40-2 it had read 40 mph. I peered through the haze of exhaust floating around the top deck covers near the exhaust manifold. Suddenly I

Washington Forest Heritage Museum at Elbe, Wash., returned F9A 838 to its original paint and numbers.
ROBERT GALLEGOS PHOTO

A string of E's retired in 1992 lines the curve under Canal Street just south of downtown Chicago.

flashed on what Brandt and Hansen had said about being trapped inside of a covered wagon when it throws a rod: "A lot of guys have come close to getting killed inside them bastards." Getting killed — even by an F unit — was more than I'd bargained for. To hell with it, I decided, and bolted out of the 769 back to the

warm, civilized cab of the trailing SD40-2.

THAT SHOULD have been my last encounter with BN's F's. Shortly after my close encounter with the 769 BN began herding the remaining F's off to scrappers for trade-in credit on new cabless GE B30-7As.

But the F9s refused to stay down for

An out-of-service
B&O bridge on the
Chicago River looks
down on an out-of-
service BN E-unit.
PAUL D. SCHNEIDER PHOTO

In late summer 1990 both units disappeared to BN's West Burlington (Iowa) shops. There they were torn down and rebuilt from the frame up with such components as new 2,000 h.p. 16-645E prime movers, AR10-D14 main generators, and D77B traction motors. An upgrade to Dash 2 electricals prompted BN to dub the units "F9-2s."

But BN had more in mind than simply converting two F's into what were essentially GP38-2s. Shortly after they emerged from the shops in October the units were ferried to Mid-American Car in Kansas City and repainted into a handsome BN paint scheme composed of generous amounts of Brunswick green and cream paint, a white roof, red pinstripes — and stainless-steel BN heralds and red and blue reproduction EMD builder's plates. These were BN's new "Executive F's," destined for use on passenger specials and other special events. The two units — now labeled BN-1 and BN-2 — made their debut on October 13-14 at the Dwight D. Eisenhower Centennial in Abilene, Kan.

BN-1 and BN-2 are based at North Kansas City along with the rest of BN's business car fleet, much of which had been repainted into the new "executive" colors by January 1, 1993. But the two F9-2s lead anything but a pampered life. It isn't unusual to find them leaning into a workaday freight train out of Kansas City when BN's motive power needs dictate their use. To the best of my knowledge, the F9-2s have yet to be pressed into freight service out of Superior. But if that ever happens, I want to be there to see the look on the faces of Arvid Brandt, John Cincoski, and everyone else at Superior who thought they'd seen the last of BN's F units.

the count. Ten of them — five cabs and five boosters — were set aside for snow-plow service as 972000-series units. Like the six F's converted in the 1970s the 10 F9s (including the 769) exchanged their green paint for MOW red and 972000-series numbers.

In 1987 cab 972568 was donated to the Inland Empire Chapter of the National Railway Historical Society and reincarnated as NP 6703A, one of several NP F9s purchased new for passenger service in 1956. But the sight of an NP F9A decked out in NP's two-tone green passenger scheme in 1987 was nothing compared to what was in store for cab 972567 and booster 972574.

AT FIRST GLANCE BN's six-axle E8s and E9s seem to have little in common with BN's four-axle F units. While the F's came from diverse origins on GN, NP, and SP&S and had spent time in freight, passenger, and maintenance-of-way service, BN's E8s and E9s came from just one railroad — the Burlington — and were strictly of passenger pedigree.

Granted, BN once fielded a fleet of 32 E7s from Burlington, GN, and — in the case of one lonely unit — SP&S. And like many of BN's F's, the E7s locked couplers with both freight and passenger trains.

But BN's E7s were ultimately short-lived; all vanished from BN rails before the railroad was a year old.

The E8s and E9s, however, were a different matter. At merger time BN's pool of E units consisted of 37 E8As and 16 E9As. Following Burlington precedent, these E's were rotated through assignments on both intercity passenger trains and Chicago-area commuter service. Former Burlington operator Clayton Getzelman once told me that the E units in stop-and-go commuter service were regularly cycled into the intercity passenger pool so that the units could

BN's E's line up for the afternoon "dinkie parade" out of downtown Chicago in 1982.
PAUL D. SCHNEIDER PHOTO

stretch their legs and, to quote Getzelman, "blow the carbon out."

In 1972 BN cheerfully sold 21 of the E8s to Amtrak. BN retained title to five E8s, but the remainder of the E8s and E9s were sold to the Western Suburban Mass Transit District, the commuter agency that had assumed commuter operations on BN's 38-mile-long Chicago-Aurora (Ill.) main. WSMTD then shipped the units off to Morrison Knudsen for rebuilding. As built the E8s were powered by a pair of 1,125 h.p. 567B engines, while the later E9s (the last E-unit model built by EMD) contained two 1,200 h.p. 567C engines. But by the time the 25 units rolled out of MK's plant at Boise, Idaho, all such distinctions had been replaced by common 12-cylinder 645 diesel engines

and new Cummins 530 k.w. HEP (head-end-power) diesel generator sets. The Cummins units, which replaced the steam boilers that the E's had been built with, provided lights, heating, and air-conditioning for the fleet of of Budd-built double-decker commuter coaches that had been part and parcel of WSMTD's purchase of BN's commuter service. Eventually four of BN's E's were rebuilt by MK and added to WSMTD's operations, bringing the fleet of E units — all dubbed "E9s" regardless of their history — to 25 units.

Unlike my experience with the last BN F9s, I never talked at length to BN mechanical department people or engineers about the E9s. And I never had a chance to be scared shirtless inside the

E7s and E8s inherited from BN predecessor CB&Q line up at Galesburg, Ill., shortly after the 1970 merger.

J. DAVID INGLES PHOTO

Morrison-Knudsen rebuilt 25 E's for BN, including this former E8A on a westbound "dinkie."

PAUL D. SCHNEIDER PHOTO

Twin diesel engines couldn't prevent BN's E's from being replaced by single-engine F40s in 1992.

PAUL D. SCHNEIDER PHOTO

engine compartment of an E9 at speed. For many years, in fact, I simply took the E's for granted. You see, for several years in the late 1970s and early 1980s I worked as a tower operator at BN's Union Avenue tower. Union Avenue's primary function was to funnel four mainline tracks from the west into two mainline tracks into Chicago

Union Station. Union Avenue is also where trains curve and head west down BN's famous "triple track" mainline. What I most remember about BN's E9s is standing at the north windows of Union Avenue to watch the E's throttle up on their way west. The guttural roar of twin 645s would shake the tower by the throat as smoke boiled

out of the E's twin exhaust stacks and dusted the windows facing the Chicago skyline. I'd crack one of the windows open and listen to the drone of the E as it headed west with an eight- or ten-car train stuffed to the luggage racks with homeward-bound commuters. Maybe the commuter E9s didn't get a chance to stretch their legs on intercity trains, but from my vantage point inside Union Avenue tower it seemed clear that they had plenty of opportunity to blow the carbon out.

The E's were a source of pride on the East End, which is what BN people called the triple-track main between Aurora and Chicago. When I asked why the BN Es hadn't been repainted into Metra paint like the E units on the Chicago & North Western lines that Metra operated, I was told, with a touch of stubborn pride, that the E's were BN units and by God, they would stay in BN paint. Indeed, not a single E9 was ever painted in Metra colors. In fact, the only significant changes to the E's paint scheme came in the mid-1970s when orange and white safety stripes were added to the nose of the E's for improved visibility.

By the late 1980s a number of wild rumors were circulating among East End employees and railfans alike about the fate of the E's. When an E was sent to Wisconsin Central's North Fond du Lac shops for body work, fans declared that the E's would be rebuilt to last another five or 10 years. The excitable editor of one railfan magazine went so far as to declare in print that BN "requires two F40s per train to replace each two-engine E unit." In truth, the lone E was patched up because, in the words of Metra spokesman Chris Knapton, "the crew got scared looking down at the holes in the cab floor

and seeing the ballast at 65 mph." And while it was comforting to some that the E9s had a spare engine to limp into town with in the event the other engine suffered a failure, the truth was that an F40 with a single reliable 645 engine was preferable to two rebuilt 645 engines that were long past their prime.

The issue was finally resolved in 1992 when Metra began taking delivery of 22 new EMD F40PH-M2s. As the new units showed up from EMD's factory in McCook, Ill. (Metra insisted that units that would be used in Illinois would be built in Illinois, not in Canada at GMLG's London, Ontario, factory), the E's shuffled off to long storage lines at 14th Street coachyards just around the corner from Union Avenue tower. When 9913 and 9900 rolled to a stop at Chicago Union Station at 7:38 a.m. on October 16, 1992, it looked like the end of the E-unit era on BN commuter trains.

But in their final hour BN's E9s proved to have more in common with their F-unit cousins than I ever would have imagined. BN cherry-picked two units — 9919 and 9920 — and set them aside to be reborn as Executive E's. It's hard to say where the E's will wind up in their new role; the Executive F's have polished the rails of Denver, Rio Grande & Western and CSX. As for me, I'm waiting for the day I can stand at the foot of Union Avenue and once again watch BN's E's roll a westbound train into the setting sun.

The sun may shine again on the flanks of a BN E-unit in passenger service.
PAUL D. SCHNEIDER PHOTO

149

THE ROSTER

AN ALL-TIME TALLY OF BN LOCOMOTIVES
1970-1993

KEY:

ALCO: Alco Products
BLW: Baldwin Locomotive Works
GE: General Electric
GEN II: Generation II
EMD: Electro Motive Division
LRC: Livingston Rebuild Center
MK: Morrison-Knudsen
VMV: VMV Enterprises

Even-numbered F units are cabs, odd-numbered are boosters

An EMD unit remanufactured by BN or a contract supplier is listed as BN or the initials of the supplier (VMV, M-K, etc.).

Locomotive numbers that have been reused on different units are shown in parentheses: ie. BN4010-4011(2) are the second units to wear these numbers.

ROAD NOS.	LOCO TYPE	BUILDER	HP	DATE BUILT	PREVIOUS OWNER	NOTES
1-3	44 TON	GE	360	1940-1941	CB&Q	
BN-1	F9A-2		2000	1990	X-NP	
BN-2	F9B-2		2000	1990	X-NP	
ET-1-ET-3	SLUGS	NP	00	1959-1965	X-NP	5.
1(2)	NW12	BN	1200	1975	X-GN	1.
5(2)	NW12	BN	1200	1975	X-GN	1.
14&19	NW12	BN	1200	1975	X-GN	1.
20-65	SW1500	EMD	1500	1968-1973	X-FRISCO	
70	SW1	EMD	600	1941	X-FRISCO	
75-79	SW1	EMD	600	1941	X-GN	
75-79(2)	SW7	EMD	1200	1950-1951	X-FRISCO	
80-83	SW1	EMD	600	1950	X-GN	
84-97	SW1	EMD	600	1939-1941	X-CB&Q	
98-99	SW8	EMD	800	1951	X-GN	
100	SW900m	EMD	900	1957	X-NP	
101	SW8	EMD	800	1953	X-GN	
102	SW1	EMD	600	1942	X-FW&D	
106	SW1200m	EMD	1200	1955	X-GN	

ROAD NOS.	LOCO TYPE	BUILDER	HP	DATE BUILT	PREVIOUS OWNER	NOTES
107	SW7	EMD	1200	1950	X-C&S	
108-114	SW7	EMD	1200	1949	X-NP	
115-134	SW7	EMD	1200	1950	X-CB&Q	
135-145	SW7	EMD	1200	1950	X-GN	
146-155	SW9	EMD	1200	1950-1951	X-GN	
150-153	NW2	EMD	1000	1947-1948	X-C&S	
154	SW70	EMD	1000	1950	X-C&S	
156-160	SW1200	EMD	1200	1959	X-C&S	
156-159	SW9	EMD	1200	1952-1953	X-NP	
160-161	SW9	EMD	1200	1951	X-CB&Q	
162-166	SW1200	EMD	1200	1957	X-GN	
167-169	SW9	EMD	1200	1951	X-SP&S	
170-228	SW1200	EMD	1200	1955-1958	X-NP	
229-238	SW1200	EMD	1200	1955	X-CB&Q	
239-250	SW1200	EMD	1200	1965	X-CB&Q	
251-255	SW1200	EMD	1200	1959	X-C&S	
256-259	SW1200	EMD	1200	1959	X-FW&D	
260-269	SW9	EMD	1200	1952	X-FRISCO	
300-309	SW1500	EMD	1500	1967	X-GN	
310-324	SW1500	EMD	1500	1973		
375-394	SW1000	EMD	1000	1972		
400-405	VO1000	BLW	1000	1941-1944	X-NP	
406	DRS4-4-15	BLW	1500	1948	X-NP	
407	DRS6-6-15	BLW	1500	1948	X-NP	
408-425	VO1000	BLW	1000	1944-1945	X-NP	
400-403(2)	NW2	EMD	1000	1947-1948	X-C&S	
405-406(2)	NW2	EMD	1000	1946	X-FW&D	
410-425(2)	NW2	EMD	1000	1948-1949	X-FRISCO	
427-449	SW1000	EMD	1000	1970-1971		2.
450-499	NW2	EMD	1000	1939-1949	X-GN	
500-573	NW2	EMD	1000	1940-1949	X-CB&Q	
574-585	SW1000	EMD	1000	1966	X-CB&Q	
586	NW2	EMD	1000	1948	X-NP	
587	NW2	EMD	1000	1941	X-FW&D	
588-592	NW2	EMD	1000	1940-1941	X-NP	
593-595	NW2	EMD	1000	1948	X-SP&S	
601-602	SW1	EMD	600	1940-1939	X-FW&D	

EMD SW1000B at Galesburg, Ill., July 1992.

JIM SHEPARD PHOTO, AUTHOR'S COLLECTION

ROAD NOS.	LOCO TYPE	BUILDER	HP	DATE BUILT	PREVIOUS OWNER	NOTES
603	NW2	EMD	1000	1941	X-FW&D	
604	SW1	EMD	600	1942	X-FW&D	
605-606	NW2	EMD	1000	1946	X-FW&D	
607-610	SW1200	EMD	1200	1959	X-FW&D	
600-604(2)	GP9B	BN	1750	1982	X-GN & NP	3. 15.
600-610	F7	EMD	1500	1950-1952	X-GN	
612, 614	F3	EMD	1500	1947	X-GN	
616	F7	EMD	1500	1950	X-GN	
618	F3	EMD	1500	1948	X-GN	
620-675	F7	EMD	1500	1950-1952	X-GN	
676, 678	F3	EMD	1500	1948	X-GN	
677	F7	EMD	1500	1952	X-GN	
680-694	F7	EMD	1500	1952-1953	X-GN	
698, 700	F7	EMD	1500	1949	X-GN	
700-703	GP7	EMD	1500	1950	X-FWD	
700(2)	F7	EMD	1500	1949	X-GN	
701-703(2)	F3	EMD	1500	1947-1948	X-NP	
701-709	F3	EMD	1500	1947-1948	X-NP	
710	F7	EMD	1500	1950	X-NP	
711	F3	EMD	1500	1947	X-NP	
712-725	F7	EMD	1500	1950	X-NP	
726	FP7	EMD	1500	1952	X-NP	
727-759	F7	EMD	1500	1950-1951	X-NP	
760	F3	EMD	1500	1948	X-NP	
761	F7	EMD	1500	1950	X-NP	
762-763	F3	EMD	1500	1948-1947	X-NP	
766-795	F9	EMD	1500	1954-1956	X-NP	
798	FT-A	EMD	1350	1945	X-NP	
799	FT-B	EMD	1350	1944	X-NP	
810-819	SD7	EMD	1500	1953	X-C&S	
820-842	SD9	EMD	1750	1956-1959	X-C&S	

ROAD NOS.	LOCO TYPE	BUILDER	HP	DATE BUILT	PREVIOUS OWNER	NOTES
868-874	SD45	EMD	3600	1971	X-C&S	
875-887	SD40	EMD	3000	1967-1968	X-C&S	
890-893	U30C	GE	3000	1968	X-C&S	
800-844	F9	EMD	1500	1954-1956	X-NP	
845-853	F9	EMD	1500	1954	X-GN	
850-859	SD7	EMD	1500	1953	X-C&S	
900-912	S2	ALCO	1000	1941-1949	X-NP	
913-924	S4	ALCO	1000	1951-1953	X-NP	
934-940	S2	ALCO	1000	1942-1943	X-SP&S	
950	S6	ALCO	800	1955	X-NP	
952-953	RS1	ALCO	1000	1945	X-NP	
986-995	NW5	EMD	1000	1946	X-GN	
1000-1004	MP15	EMD	1500	1975	X-FRISCO	
1100-1101	SL-144	GE	1150	1981		
1350-1365	GP5	EMD	1500	1959	X-GN	
1375-1399	GP15-1	EMD	1500	1977	X-FRISCO	
1400-1438	GP10	EMD	1800	1974-1976		4.
1500-1555	GP7	EMD	1500	1950-1953	X-GN	
1556-1623	GP7	EMD	1500	1951-1952	X-CB&Q	
1624-1643	GP7	EMD	1500	1951-1953	X-NP	
1670-1673	GP7	EMD	1500	1950	X-FW&D	
1500-1523(2)	GP28M	M-K	1600	1990-		
1700-1760	GP9	EMD	1750	1954-1958	X-NP	
1776(2)	U30C	GE	3000	1972		26.
1761-1839	GP9	EMD	1750	1954-1958	X-GN	

GE U30C 892 at Cicero, Ill., September 1973.

PAUL D. SCHNEIDER PHOTO

1840-1954	GP9	EMD	1750	1955-1958	X-NP	
1876(2)	SD40-2	EMD	3000	1972		26.
1955-1974	GP9	EMD	1750	1954	X-CB&Q	
1975-1980	GP9	EMD	1750	1955-1956	X-SP&S	
1976(2)	SDP40	EMD	3000	1966		26.
1990-1998	GP18	EMD	1800	1960	X-NP	

ROAD NOS.	LOCO TYPE	BUILDER	HP	DATE BUILT	PREVIOUS OWNER	NOTES
1991(2)	SD60M	EMD	3800	1991		
2000-2035	GP20	EMD	2000	1960	X-GN	HIGH NOSE
2036-2071	GP20	EMD	2000	1961	X-CB&Q	LOW NOSE
2000(2)	GP20C	GEN II	2000	1989		5.-RETIRED
2001-2009(2)	GP20C	GEN II	2000	1989-1990		5.
2072-2077	GP38	EMD	2000	1970	X-SP&S	22.
2078-2109	GP38-2	EMD	2000	1972-1974		
2110-2138	GP38AC	EMD	2000	1971	X-FRISCO	
2150-2154	GP38-2	EMD	2000	1980	X-FW&D	
2155-2189	GP38X	EMD	2000	1970	X-CR(PC)	
2200-2216	GP30	EMD	2250	1963	X-GN	
2217-2254	GP30	EMD	2250	1962-1963	X-CB&Q	
2255-2369	GP38-2	EMD	2000	1972-1976	X-FRISCO	
2500-2523	GP35	EMD	2500	1964-1965	X-GN	
2524-2545	GP35	EMD	2500	1963-1964	X-CB&Q	
2550-2582	GP35	EMD	2500	1964-1965	X-FRISCO	
2600	GP38B	BN	2000	1981		15.
2601	GP38-2B	BN	2000	1981		15.
2700-2739	GP39-2	EMD	2300	1981		
2750-2778	GP39E	EMD	2300	1989-1991		6.
2800-2834	GP39M	M-K	2300	1988-1990		7.
2874-2886	GP39M	M-K	2300	1988-1991		8.
2900-2940	GP39E	EMD	2300	1989-1990		9.
2960-2984	GP39V	VMV	2300	1990		10.
3000-3039	GP40	EMD	3000	1966-1968	X-CB&Q	
3040-3064	GP40-2	EMD	3000	1979	X-FRISCO	
3075-3084	GP40	EMD	3000	1989	X-CSXT	
3100-3109	GP50	EMD	3500	1980	X-FRISCO	11.
3110-3162	GP50	EMD	3500	1985		12.
3500-3523	GP40M	M-K	3000	1988-1989		13.
3550-3555	GP40E	EMD	3000	1989		14.

BN-rebuilt GP7 1426 at New Westminster, B.C., October 1978.
PAUL D. SCHNEIDER PHOTO

GE U30C 1776(2nd) at Denver, Colo., March 1977.
JAMES P. MARCUS, AUTHOR'S COLLECTION

ROAD NOS.	LOCO TYPE	BUILDER	HP	DATE BUILT	PREVIOUS OWNER	NOTES
4000-4002	RS2	ALCO	1500	1949-1950	X-SP&S	
4010-4011	C415	ALCO	1500	1968	X-SP&S	
4050-4078	RS3	ALCO	1600	1950-1953	X-SP&S	
4081-4086	RS3	ALCO	1600	1955	X-NP	
4100, 4102	FA1	ALCO	1500	1949	X-SP&S	
4104, 4106	FA1	ALCO	1500	1949	X-SP&S	
4108	FA1	ALCO	1500	1949	X-SP&S	
4112, 4114	FA1	ALCO	1500	1948	X-GN	
4116, 4118	FA1	ALCO	1500	1949	X-GN	
4120, 4122	FA1	ALCO	1500	1950	X-SP&S	
4126	FA2	ALCO	1600	1950	X-SP&S	
4000-4002(2)	MP15	EMD	1500	1975	X-FRISCO	RE#1000-1002
4003-4004	MP15	EMD	1500	1975	X-FRISCO	RE#1003-1004
4000-4002(3)	B30-7A	GE	3000	1982		15.
4003-4004(2)	B30-7A	GE	3000	1982		15.
4005-4009	B30-7A	GE	3000	1982		15.
4010-4011(2)	B30-7A	GE	3000	1982		15.
4012-4049	B30-7A	GE	3000	1982		15.
4050-4052(2)	B30-7A	GE	3000	1982		15.
4053-4078(2)	B30-7A	GE	3000	1983		15.
4079-4080	B30-7A	GE	3000	1983		15.
4081-4086(2)	B30-7A	GE	3000	1983		15.
4087-4099	B30-7A	GE	3000	1983		15.
4100,4102(2)	B30-7A	GE	3000	1983		15.
4101,4103	B30-7A	GE	3000	1983		15.
4104,4106(2)	B30-7A	GE	3000	1983		15.
4105,4107	B30-7A	GE	3000	1983		15.
4109-4111	B30-7A	GE	3000	1983		15.
4108,4112(2)	B30-7A	GE	3000	1983		15.
4113,4115	B30-7A	GE	3000	1983		15.
4114,4116(2)	B30-7A	GE	3000	1983		15.

ROAD NOS.	LOCO TYPE	BUILDER	HP	DATE BUILT	PREVIOUS OWNER	NOTES
4118(2)	B30-7A	GE	3000	1983		15.
4117,4119	B30-7A	GE	3000	1983		15.
4180-4197	RS11	ALCO	1800	1958-1960		
4240-4246	C424	ALCO	2400	1964	X-SP&S	
4250-4265	C425	ALCO	2500	1965-1966	X-SP&S	
4360-4369	C636	ALCO	3600	1968	X-SP&S	
4500	U30C	BN	3000	1983		15.
5000-5141	C30-7	GE	3000	1979-1981		
5200-5208	U23C	GE	2250	1969	X-GN	
5210-5233	U25B	GE	2500	1963-1966	X-FRISCO	
5300-5305	U30C	GE	3000	1972		RE#5800-5805
5300-5305(2)	U30C	GE	3000	1975		
5306-5352	U30C	GE	3000	1972		
5353-5364	U30C	GE	3000	1972		RE#5900-5911
5353-5364(2)	U30C	GE	3000	1975		
5365-5394	U30C	GE	3000	1974		
5396-5399	U30C	GE	3000	1968	X-C&S	
5400-5423	U25B	GE	2500	1964-1965	X-GN	
5424-5429	U25B	GE	2500	1964	X-CB&Q	
5450-5459	U28B	GE	2800	1966-1967	X-CB&Q	
5460-5465	U28B	GE	2800	1966	X-GN	
5470-5484	U30B	GE	3000	1966-1968	X-CB&Q	
5485-5492	B30-7	GE	3000	1977	X-FRISCO	
5497-5499	B32-8	GE	3150	1984		
5500-5599	C30-7	GE	3000	1976-1979		
5600-5629	U25C	GE	2500	1964-1965	X-NP	
5630-5641	U25C	GE	2500	1965	X-CB&Q	
5650-5665	U28C	GE	2800	1966	X-CB&Q	
5666-5677	U28C	GE	2800	1966	X-NP	
5700-5714	U33C	GE	3300	1968-1969	X-GN	
5715-5724	U33C	GE	3300	1969	X-NP	
5725-5728	U33C	GE	3300	1971	X-CB&Q	23.
5729-5763	U33C	GE	3300	1971		
5764-5765	U33C	GE	3300	1969	X-S.J. GROVES	
5770-5781	U30B	GE	3000	1968-1969	X-FRISCO	
5782-5799	U30B	GE	3000	1973-1975	X-FRISCO	
5800-5805	U30C	GE	3000	1972	X-BN 5300-5305(1)	
5806-5839	U30C	GE	3000	1973-1975		
5900-5911	U30C	GE	3000	1972	X-BN-5353-5364(1)	
5912-5944	U30C	GE	3000	1973-1975		
6000-6022	SD7	EMD	1500	1952-1953	X-GN	
6023-6059	SD7	EMD	1500	1952-1953	X-CB&Q	
6070-6079	SD7	EMD	1500	1953	X-C&S	
6080-6089	SD7	EMD	1500	1953	X-FW&D	
6100-6126	SD9	EMD	1750	1954-1958	X-GN	
6127-6206	SD9	EMD	1750	1954-1957	X-CB&Q	
6215-6237	SD9	EMD	1750	1956-1959	X-C&S	
6240-6255	SD24	EMD	2400	1959	X-CB&Q	
6240-6247(2)	SD9	LRC	1750	1989-1990		16.

ROAD NOS.	LOCO TYPE	BUILDER	HP	DATE BUILT	PREVIOUS OWNER	NOTES
6260-6263	SD38-2	EMD	2000	1979	X-FRISCO	
6266	SD38P	VMV	2000	1992-1993		17.
6291	TEBC6	VMV	00	1992-1993		18.
6300-6324	SD40	EMD	3000	1971		
6325-6329	SD40-2	EMD	3000	1972		
6330	SD40-2	EMD	3000	1972		
6330(2)	SD40-2	BN	3600	1986		CAT ENGINE
6331-6334	SD40-2	EMD	3000	1972		
6335-6339	SD40-2	EMD	3000	1972		RE#6912-6916
6335-6339(2)	SD40	EMD	3000	1967-1968	X-C&S	
6340-6347	SD40-2	EMD	3000	1973		RE#6800-6807
6340-6347(2)	SD40	EMD	3000	1967-1968	X-C&S	
6348-6363	SD40-2	EMD	3000	1973		RE#6808-6823
6348-6363(2)	SD40-2	EMD	3000	1972-1974	X-C&S	
6364-6375	SD40-2	EMD	3000	1972-1974		RE#6900-6911
6364-6375(2)	SD40-2	EMD	3000	1972-1974		
6376-6385	SD40-2	EMD	3000	1974		
6394-6399	SDP40	EMD	3000	1966	X-GN	
6400-6429	SD45	EMD	3600	1966-1968	X-NP	

GE U28C 5674 on lease to DOT at Galesburg, Ill., May 1971.
CARL F. NELSON PHOTO, F. HOL WAGNER, JR. COLLECTION

ROAD NOS.	LOCO TYPE	BUILDER	HP	DATE BUILT	PREVIOUS OWNER	NOTES
6430-6456	SD45	EMD	3600	1966-1968	X-GN	
6457-6471	SD45	EMD	3600	1969	X-CB&Q	
6472-6483	SD45	EMD	3600	1970	X-NP	
6484-6491	SD45	EMD	3600	1970	X-NP	24.
6492-6497	SD45	EMD	3600	1970	X-CB&Q	23.
6498-6567	SD45	EMD	3600	1971		
6570-6576	SD45	EMD	3600	1971	X-C&S	
6592-6599	SDP45	EMD	3600	1967	X-GN	
6600-6613	F45	EMD	3600	1969	X-GN	
6614-6625	F45	EMD	3600	1970	X-GN	25.
6626-6646	F45	EMD	3600	1971		
6650-6696	SD45	EMD	3600	1967-1969	X-FRISCO	

EMD SD45 6430 at Denver, Colo., May 1974.

F. HOL WAGNER, JR. PHOTO

ROAD NOS.	LOCO TYPE	BUILDER	HP	DATE BUILT	PREVIOUS OWNER	NOTES
6700-6799	SD40-2	EMD	3000	1974-1977		
6800-6823	SD40-2	EMD	3000	1973	X-BN 6340(1)-6363(1)	
6824-6836	SD40-2	EMD	3000	1973		
6840-6847	SD40-2	EMD	3000	1978	X-FRISCO	
6850	SD40-2	EMD	3000	1974	X-C&S	
6900-6911	SD40-2	EMD	3000	1973-1974	X-BN 6364(1)-6375(1)	
6912-6916	SD40-2	EMD	3000	1972	X-BN 6335(1)-6339(1)	
6917-6928	SD40-2	EMD	3000	1973		
6950	SD40-2	EMD	3000	1974	X-C&S	
7000-7048	SD40-2	EMD	3000	1977-1978		
7049-7053	SD40-2SS	EMD	3000	1978		
7054-7148	SD40-2	EMD	3000	1978-1979		
7149	SD40-2 LNG	CEECO	3000	1992		19.
7150-7291	SD40-2	EMD	3000	1979-1980		
7300-7309	SD40	EMD	3000	1989	X-MP	
7500-7502	SD40-2B	BN	3000	1981-1984		15.
7600	SD40B	BN	3000	1981		15.
7800-7889	SD40-2	EMD	3000	1974-1979	X-C&S	
7890	SD40-2LNG	CEECO	3000	1991		19.
7891-7940	SD40-2	EMD	3000	1979-1980	X-C&S	
8000-8181	SD40-2	EMD	3000	1977-1980		
8300-8302	SD60	EMD	3800	1985		
8500-8599	B39-8E	GE	3900	1978-1988		20.
9000-9099	SD60	EMD	3800	1986		21.
9200-9298	SD60M	EMD	3800	1989-1991		
9500-9503	SD60MAC	EMD	3800	1992		
9700, 9703	F3	EMD	1500	1947	X-GN	
9702, 9709	F7	EMD	1500	1952	X-GN	
9705-9708	F3	EMD	1500	1947	X-GN	
9710-9711	F7	EMD	1500	1946-1947	X-GN	
9712	F7	EMD	1500	1952	X-GN	
9713-9716	F3	EMD	1500	1947	X-GN	
9717-9728	F7	EMD	1500	1950, 1953	X-GN	

ROAD NOS.	LOCO TYPE	BUILDER	HP	DATE BUILT	PREVIOUS OWNER	NOTES
9729-9733	F3	EMD	1500	1947-1948	X-GN	
9735-9749	F7	EMD	1500	1950-1953	X-GN	
9750, 9752	F3	EMD	1500	1947, 1949	X-SP&S	
9762-9763	F3	EMD	1500	1947	X-NP	
9764,	F7	EMD	1500	1949	X-NP	
9765-9766	F3	EMD	1500	1947	X-NP	
9767-9774	F7	EMD	1500	1949-1950	X-NP	
9775, 9777	F3	EMD	1500	1947	X-NP	
9776,	F7	EMD	1500	1949	X-NP	
9778-9790	F7	EMD	1500	1949-1950	X-NP	
9792, 9794	FP7	EMD	1500	1952	X-NP	
9800-9830	F9	EMD	1750	1954-1956	X-NP	
9850-9855	SDP40	EMD	3000	1966	X-GN	
9856-9863	SDP45	EMD	3600	1967	X-GN	
9900	E7	EMD	2000	1948	X-SP&S	
9901-9910	E7	EMD	2000	1945-1947	X-GN	
9911-9931	E7	EMD	2000	1945-1949	X-CB&Q	
9932-9977	E8A	EMD	2250	1949-1953	X-CB&Q	
9980-9995	E9A	EMD	2250	1954-1956	X-CB&Q	
9900-9904(2)	E8Au	M-K	2400	1973-1974		
9905-9908(2)	E8Au	M-K	2400	1978		
9910-9925(2)	E9Au	M-K	2400	1973		

NOTES

1. REBUILT BY BN FROM X-GN UNITS
2. #442 REBUILT BY BN WITHOUT A CAB
3. REBUILT BY NP FROM BALDWIN SWITCHERS
4. REBUILT BY BN FROM GN, NP, & CB&Q GP7's.
5. REBUILT BY GEN II FROM GN & CB&Q GP20's.
6. REBUILT BY EMD FROM GN, CB&Q, CSXT, & UP GP30's.
7. REBUILT BY M-K FROM GN, CB&Q, UP, CSXT, & SSW GP30's.
8. REBUILT BY M-K FROM GN, CB&Q, FRISCO, SSW & SP GP35's.
9. REBUILT BY EMD FROM FRISCO, MP, UP, GN, & CB&Q GP35's.
10. REBUILT BY VMV FROM SP, CSXT, ICG, & GM&O, GP35'S
11. ORDERED BY FRISCO - DELIVERED TO BN
12. 3158-3162 5-PERSON CAB - LAST PRODUCTION GP50's
13. REBUILT BY M-K FROM CB&Q GP40's
14. REBUILT BY EMD FROM CB&Q GP40's
15. CABLESS UNITS
16. REBUILT BY LRC IN LIVINGSTON, MONTANA FROM DM&IR & CSXT SD9's
17. REBUILT BY VMV
18. REBUILT BY VMV
19. REFRIGERATED LIGUIFIED METHANE-FUELED
20. POWER BY THE HOUR UNITS FROM LMX
21. POWER BY THE HOUR UNITS FROM OAKWAY
22. ORDERED BY SP&S - DELIVERED TO BN
23. ORDERED BY CB&Q - DELIVERED TO BN
24. ORDERED BY NP - DELIVERED TO BN
25. ORDERED BY GN - DELIVERED TO BN
26. PAINTED FOR 1976 BICENTENNIAL

PRE-MERGER LOCOMOTIVES STILL ON THE ROSTER

AS OF 1/01/93:

ROAD NOS.	LOCO TYPE	BUILDER	HP	DATE BUILT	PREVIOUS OWNER	NOTES
20-65	SW1500	EMD	1500	1968-1973	X-FRISCO	
70	SWI	EMD	600	1941	X-FRISCO	
162-166	SW1200	EMD	1200	1957	X-GN	LESS#165
169	SW9	EMD	1200	1951	X-SP&S	
574-585	SW1000	EMD	1000	1966	X-CB&Q	
1000-1004	MP15	EMD	1500	1975	X-FRISCO	
1375-1399	GP15-1	EMD	1500	1977	X-FRISCO	
1702-1734	GP9	EMD	1750	1954-1957	X-NP	
1742-1764	GP9	EMD	1750	1957-1955	X-NP	
1783-1800	GP9	EMD	1750	1956-1958	X-GN	
1802-1804	GP9	EMD	1750	1958	X-GN	
1811-1813	GP9	EMD	1750	1954	X-GN	
1816-1819	GP9	EMD	1750	1954	X-GN	
1821-1829	GP9	EMD	1750	1954	X-GN	
1841-1854	GP9	EMD	1750	1955	X-NP	
1858-1863	GP9	EMD	1750	1955	X-NP	
1861-1868	GP9	EMD	1750	1955-1956	X-NP	
1875-1883	GP9	EMD	1750	1956	X-NP	
1877-1898	GP9	EMD	1750	1956	X-NP	
1913-1922	GP9	EMD	1750	1957	X-NP	
1916-1917	GP9	EMD	1750	1957	X-NP	

EMD GP9 1714 at Minneapolis, Minn., July 1972.

PAUL D. SCHNEIDER PHOTO

ROAD NOS.	LOCO TYPE	BUILDER	HP	DATE BUILT	PREVIOUS OWNER	NOTES
1938-1954	GP9	EMD	1750	1958	X-NP	
1958-1965	GP9	EMD	1750	1954	X-CB&Q	
1969-1971	GP9	EMD	1750	1954	X-CB&Q	
1977	GP9	EMD	1750	1956-1955	X-SP&S	
2030-2031	GP20	EMD	2000	1960	X-GN	
2044-2048	GP20	EMD	2000	1961	X-CB&Q	
2049-2054	GP20	EMD	2000	1961	X-CB&Q	
2057-2058	GP20	EMD	2000	1961	X-CB&Q	

EMD SW1 70 at Memphis, Tenn., April 1982.

LON COONE PHOTO, AUTHOR'S COLLECTION

EMD SDP40 6399 at Denver, Colo., January 1991.
RICHARD LOUDERBACK PHOTO, AUTHOR'S COLLECTION

ROAD NOS.	LOCO TYPE	BUILDER	HP	DATE BUILT	PREVIOUS OWNER	NOTES
2063	GP20	EMD	2000	1961	X-CB&Q	
2110-2138	GP38AC	EMD	2000	1971	X-FRISCO	
2255-2369	GP38-2	EMD	2000	1972-1976	X-FRISCO	
2543	GP35	EMD	2500	1964	X-CB&Q	
3040-3064	GP40-2	EMD	3000	1979	X-FRISCO	
5485-5492	B30-7	GE	3000	1977	X-FRISCO	
5797	U30B	GE	3000	1975	X-FRISCO	
6100-6103	SD9	EMD	1750	1954	X-GN	
6107-6110	SD9	EMD	1750	1956	X-GN	
6113-6123	SD9	EMD	1750	1957-1958	X-GN	
6125-6126	SD9	EMD	1750	1958	X-GN	

ROAD NOS.	LOCO TYPE	BUILDER	HP	DATE BUILT	PREVIOUS OWNER	NOTES
6127-6139	SD9	EMD	1750	1954	X-CB&Q	
6133-6135	SD9	EMD	1750	1954	X-CB&Q	
6141-6143	SD9	EMD	1750	1954	X-CB&Q	
6145-6146	SD9	EMD	1750	1954	X-CB&Q	
6150	SD9	EMD	1750	1955	X-CB&Q	
6152-6154	SD9	EMD	1750	1955	X-CB&Q	
6156-6158	SD9	EMD	1750	1955	X-CB&Q	
6160-6162	SD9	EMD	1750	1955	X-CB&Q	
6164-6167	SD9	EMD	1750	1955	X-CB&Q	
6176-6178	SD9	EMD	1750	1955-1957	X-CB&Q	
6181	SD9	EMD	1750	1957	X-CB&Q	
6183-6185	SD9	EMD	1750	1957	X-CB&Q	
6190-6192	SD9	EMD	1750	1957	X-CB&Q	
6194-6199	SD9	EMD	1750	1957	X-CB&Q	
6204	SD9	EMD	1750	1957	X-CB&Q	
6217-6218	SD9	EMD	1750	1956	X C&S	
6221	SD9	EMD	1750	1956	X C&S	
6223-6224	SD9	EMD	1750	1957	X C&S	
6226-6228	SD9	EMD	1750	1959	X C&S	
6230-6237	SD9	EMD	1750	1959	X C&S	
6260-6263	SD38-2	EMD	2000	1979	X-FRISCO	
6339(2)	SD40	EMD	3000	1968	X-C&S	
6397-6399	SDP40	EMD	3000	1966	X-GN	
6840-6847	SD40-2	EMD	3000	1978	X-FRISCO	
6850	SD40-2	EMD	3000	1974	X-C&S	
6950	SD40-2	EMD	3000	1974	X-C&S	
7800-7889	SD40-2	EMD	3000	1974-1979	X-C&S	
7891-7923	SD40-2	EMD	3000	1979	X-C&S	

EMD SD9 6157 at Eola, Ill., January 1980.
PAUL D. SCHNEIDER PHOTO

INDEX

A

AC traction, 71-75, 83
Air Products & Chemicals, 78
Alarm bells, 84
Alco, 10
  defunct, 33
Alco AAR Type B trucks, 91, 128
Alco FAs, 14, 17, 18, 19, 21, 91
Alco switchers, 119
  reengined by Frisco, 128
  repowered, 101
Amtrak
  fuel tender concept, 114
  passenger service and, 20, 135
  purchase of E units, 144
Anderson, Andy, 26
Arkansas and Missouri, 11
Auburn terminal, 84

B

B30-7As, 42
  cabless, 106, 109
B39-8s, 60
Baldwin, 10, 120
  switchers rebuilt, 104
Belknap Yard, 132
Berwind Railway Services, 115
Big bombers, 60
  technology, 83
BL20, 96
Blomberg trucks, 92, 94, 98
Brandt, Arvin, 137-39, 142
Burlington, 10
  E units and, 143
Burlington Northern

AC traction, 74, 75
alternative locomotives, 88
assignment of locomotives, 84, 86
assimilating others' locomotives, 116
big bomber locomotives, 60
business car fleet, 142
cabless units and, 108
competitive remanufacturing, 91
cost of alternate fuel engines, 82
costs of cabs, 109
failed repower attempts, 101
formation of, 8
fuel costs, 83, 115
fuel tenders, 113, 114
F units, 120, 124
halting of retirements, 49
headquarters relocate, 12, 13
leasing locomotives, 46, 62, 101
locomotive fleet, 131
low horsepower branchline locomotive, 97
maintenance, 63, 67
mergers, 11, 108, 134
natural gas program, 81
ordering cabless locomotive, 109
painting, 67, 68
passenger service and, 20
power acquisitions, 60, 62
power by the hour, 67, 75
power shortage, 28, 31, 134
rebuilding wrecked locomotives, 108
remanufacturing of locomotives,
  50, 53, 95
retirement of locomotives, 34
second-generation engine retirements, 44
source of revenue, 13
spin off of A&M, 11
updating locomotives, 39
working with EMD, 69

yard slugs, 104-106

C

C30-7s, 28, 36
C424s, 58
C636s, 60
Cab unit carbodies, 19
Calumet Yard, 5, 54
Cargill Grain Co, 25
Caterpillar, 98, 101, 102
Century series road switchers, 30
Chicago & North Western, 149
  fight with BN over Powder River
    Basin, 11
  repowering road switchers, 101
Chicago, Burlington & Quincy, 8, 116
Chicago Region, 30, 31
Chopped noses, 90
Cicero Yard, 54
Cincoski, John, 137, 139, 143
Cle Elum Turn, 84, 86, 113
Cliffs Western Australia Mining, 35
Colorado & Southern, 125
  absorption by BN, 11
  SD40s, 127
Comprehensive Locomotive Rebuild
  Program (CLRP), 88
Converted F7s (CF7s), 28
Covered wagons, 19, 26, 44, 132
  problems with, 137
  See also F units
CP Rail, AC traction and, 73
Crawford Hill, 125
Critters, 76
CSXT, 55, 95
Cummins units, 144

D

Dash 2, 57, 97
  upgrade in GP30s, 91
  upgrade of F9s, 142
Dash 7, 39, 128
DC series traction motors, 71
Denver Region, 115
Deregulation, 11
Diesel oil, 75, 76
Double-stack trains, 54
Drag units, 113
Drury, George H., 8
Duluth, Missabe & Iron Range, 106
  ET-3, 106
Dynamic brakes, 94

E

East End, 149
Eisenhower, Dwight D., Centennial, 142
Electric power, 77, 78
Electric trailers. See Yard slugs
Electro Northern, 64
  feedback to EMD, 65
EMD, 10, 10, 95
  building SD45s, 17, 17
  dominance of market, 35
  E units, 20
  FLexicoil trucks, 55, 112
  F units and, 19, 28, 42, 107
  GP switchers, 20
  hood units, 138
  leases with, 62
  link with Electro Northern, 64
  maintenance and, 69
  parts inventory, 41
  profit margin, 87
  remanufacturing of locomotives, 50
  SD switchers, 20
  self-steering, 111
  See also the specific engine number
EMD GP50s, 42
Employee relations, 10, 11
ET-1, 104, 107
ET-2, 104, 107
ET-3, 104, 106, 107
E units, 20, 128, 143, 147
  commuter service, 143

F

F3Bs, 108
F3 cab unit, 22
F3s, 58
  retirement of, 41
F40s, fuel needs of, 114
F45s
  resold, 47
  retirement of, 44
F6Bs, 108
F7s, retirement of, 41
F9 cabs, 42
F9s, 26
FAs, 124
  retirement of, 33
Federal Railroad Administration,
  63, 78, 137
Flange lubrication, 115
Fort Worth & Denver, 11
Frisco, 116, 127
  merger with BN, 11, 128
  traded in FAs, 91, 92
  use of SDP45s, 19
FT 103 (road diesel), 107
Fuel, diesel, 75
  alternatives, 77, 78, 81
  costs, 83, 115
  economies, 99
   versus gas, 76
  supply, 76, 77
Fuel tenders, 110, 113-15
  construction of, 114-15
  converted to tank cars, 115
  structural problems, 115
  tests of, 115
F units, 19, 20, 28, 84, 120, 128, 132
  cabless boosters, 107
  exodus of, 40
  overhaul of, 135
  owned by BN, 124
  part of carbody, 137
  power shortage and, 31, 134
  problems with, 137, 139-41
  retirement of, 134
  snowplow service, 142

G

GE, 10, 28
  Dash 7 improvements, 39
  dominance of market, 30
  leases with, 62
  study of power source, 77
General Motors Locomotive Group
  (GMLG), 65, 67, 110, 149
Generation II Locomotive, 98, 101, 102
Getzelman, Clayton, 143
GP15s, 128
GP20C project, 98-99
GP20s
  high nose, 125
  low nose, 125
  retirement, 44
GP30s, 50, 91
GP35s, kept by BN, 50
GP38-2, 86
GP38s, ordered for local service, 86
GP39-2s, 87
GP40s
  kept by BN, 50
  in remanufacturing program, 94
GP7s
  purge of, 41
  rebuilt, 88
GP9s
  rebuilt as cabless units, 108
  remanufacturing of, 53
  still used by BN, 50
Grand Trunk Western, 101
Great Northern, 8
  assimilating locomotives into BN, 116
  former units of, 90
  high nose units, 98
  recycling components and, 23
Gulf, Mobile & Ohio, 91, 96

H

H. K. Porter, Inc., 76
Hansen, Jim, 137, 138, 139
Hart, Steve, 106
Head-end power, 21
Helm Leasing (HLC), 49
Hill, Gene, 132
Hood unit, 19, 20
HTBB truck, 70, 110

HTCR, 70
Hyman-Michaels Co., 25

I

Illinois Central Gulf, 94, 95
Inland Empire Chapter of the National
  Railway Historical Society, 142

J

Johnson, Jerry, 132
Joseph Simon & Sons of Tacoma, 21

K

Kato, 99
Kiamichi Railroad, 12
Knapton, Chris, 149

L

Lake Superior & Ishpeming, 47
Levin, Fred, 139
Liquid propane gas (LPG), 80, 81
LMX, 60
Locomotives, 8
  alarm bells, 84
  assimilation of, 116
  big bombers, 60
  cost of cabs, 107
  electric, 78
  engine life, 82
  fleet of, 10, 131
  fuel, 76, 77
  fuel tenders and, 114
  gasoline, 76
  head-end power, 21
  high horsepower, 40, 46, 47
    failed repowerings, 101
  leasing of, 62
  low horsepower, 97
  medium horsepower, 87, 98
  painting of, 65, 116, 118
  power sources, 70-72
  price of, 88
  remanufacturing of, 50
  renumbering of, 10, 10, 65, 116, 118, 131,

  134
  repowering, difficulties in, 102
  retirement of, 14, 19, 26, 34
    changing of, 57
    halted, 49
  RLM-fueled engines, 83
  second-generation retirements, 44-49
  trade-ins, 22, 23
Long Island Rail Road, 21
Los Alamos-National Laboratory, 80
Louisville & Nashville, ACL unit, 94

M

Metra, 149
Mid-American Car, 142
Montana Rail Link, 12, 49
Morgan, David P., 40
Morrison Knudsen, 95, 144
Motors, 70-72
MP15s, 128
Murray Yard, 64

N

National Railway Leasing (NRL), 49
Natural gas, 76-78, 81
  costs, 83
  testing of, 80
New York, Ontario & Western Railway,
  25
New York, Susquehanna & Western, 49
Norfolk Southern, 13
  double-stack transfers, 54
Northern Pacific (NP), 118
Northern Pacific, 8, 137
  assimilating locomotives into BN, 116
  F9s and, 28
  merger with BN, 120
  rebuilt hulks, 104
Northtown Yard, 135
NW2 switchers
  acquired by BN, 124
  purge of, 41
  rebuilt, 90
NW5s
  Great Northern and, 127
  purge of, 41

O

Oakway, 60
  units maintained by EMD, 64
Operator's shelter, 108

P

Pacific Zip, 17
Portland Division, 26
Powder River Basin, 86, 87
  new units for coal service, 90
Power by the hour, 62, 63, 67, 75, 83
Power packs, 21
Propp, Dale H., 101
Push-pull trains, 21

R

Railroad Days, 96
Refrigerated liquid methane (RLM),
  78, 80
  debut, 82
  fuel, 83
  fuel tenders and, 115
Reliance Electric, 99
Remanufacturing program, 91, 94
Reservation tower, 18, 19
Roof-mounted air reservoir tanks,
  91, 128
RS11s, 34
  preferred by NP, 118
RS2s, 19
RS3s, 19

S

Santa Fe
  cab amenities, 107
  rebuilding cabless locomotives, 108
  repowering road switchers, 101
SD24s, 125
  retired in 1982, 40
SD35s
  rebuilt into yard slugs, 55
  upgraded, 57
SD38-2s, Frisco units, 128
SD38-2s, rebuilt into yard slugs, 55
SD40-2s, 28, 36

SD40s, retirement of, 44
SD45s, 16, 17, 22, 60
  and fuel, 49
  resold, 47
  retirement of, 44
SD60MACs, 70
  leap forward, 75
SD60Ms, 60, 60
SD60s, feedback on, 65
SD70MACs, 75
SD7s
  former GN engine, 118
  purge of, 41
SD9s
  rebuilt as yard slugs, 53
  in scrapyards, 57
  still used by BN, 50
SDP40s
  retirement of, 44
  steam generators, 127
SDP45s
  BN retirement of, 44
  Great Northern and, 127
  as whips, 49
Seattle-Portland Region, 28
  F units and, 135
Self-steering. See HTCR
Shoto, Archie, 13
Soo Line, concern for pollutants, 101
Southern Pacific, 91, 135
  eliminating F units, 28
Spokane, Portland & Seattle, 8, 19, 116
  contributing S1, 122

merger with BN, 122
St. Louis-San Francisco. See Frisco
Stampede Pass, 84, 113
Super cab, 67
SW1s, purge of, 41
SW7s, delay in retiring, 42
SW9s, delay in retiring, 42
Swearengin, Ron, 74
Switching locomotives, 76

T

Tank cars, conversion from fuel tenders, 115
TEBC6, 55, 57
  See also Yard slug
Transfer trains, 54, 55
Twin Cities Region, 115
  F units and, 135, 137

U

U.S. Department of Energy, 76
U23Cs, 125
  retirement of, 44
U25Bs, 39
  launch of, 40
U25Cs, retirement of, 35
U28Bs, 39
  retirement of, 44
U28Cs, retirement of, 35
U30Bs, retiring of, 44

U30Cs, 28, 58, 125
  returned by BN, 46
U33Cs, 60
  retirement of, 44
Union Avenue tower, 146
Union Pacific
  cabless concept, 107
  eliminating F units, 28
  fight over Powder River with BN, 11
Union Station, 147, 149
Unit trains, 13

V

VMV Enterprises, 53-55

W

Washington Central, 12
Western Suburban Mass Transit
  District, 144
Wisconsin Central, 49

Y

Yard slugs, 53, 54, 104

Z

Ziegler Inc., 98